VICTORIAN LITERATURE AND CULTURE

INTRODUCTIONS TO BRITISH LITERATURE AND CULTURE SERIES

Introductions to British Literature and Culture are practical guides to key literary periods. Guides in the series are designed to help introduce a new module or area of study, providing concise information on the historical, literary and critical contexts and acting as an initial map of the knowledge needed to study the literature and culture of a specific period. Each guide includes an overview of the historical period, intellectual contexts, major genres, critical approaches and a guide to original research and resource materials in the area, enabling students to progress confidently to further study.

Available also from Continuum

Medieval Literature and Culture by Andrew Galloway

Renaissance Literature and Culture by Matthew Steggle and Lisa Hopkins

Seventeenth-Century Literature and Culture by Jim Daems

Eighteenth-Century Literature and Culture by Paul Goring

Victorian Literature and Culture by Maureen Moran

Romanticism by Sharon Ruston

Modernism by Leigh Wilson

Postwar British Literature and Culture 1945–1980 by Susan Brook

Contemporary British Literature and Culture by Sean Matthews

VICTORIAN LITERATURE AND CULTURE

Maureen Moran

continuum

Continuum International Publishing Group

The Tower Building
11 York Road
London SE1 7NX

80 Maiden Lane
Suite 704
New York NY 10038

www.continuumbooks.com

© Maureen Moran 2006

First published 2006
Reprinted 2009, 2011 (twice)

British Library Cataloguing-in-Publication Data
A catalogue record for this book is available from the British Library.

ISBN: 978-08264-8883-1 (hardback)
      978-08264-8884-8 (paperback)

Library of Congress Cataloging-in-Publication Data
A catalog record for this book is available from the Library of Congress.

Typeset by Servis Filmsetting Ltd, Manchester
Printed and bound in Great Britain

Contents

Acknowledgements

This book owes a great debt to the many colleagues and friends who have fostered my love of Victorian literature and culture. In particular, I would like to thank Pete Smith, with whom I have taught many Victorian courses and from whom I have learned much – about students and about the nineteenth century. Over the years, my many students in Victorian literature classes have kept me on my mettle, and prompted me to see new connections. The encouragement of Anna Sandeman and the suggestions of the anonymous reader at Continuum have been invaluable. Linda Anderson has helped in important ways too numerous to list; and the support of the merry band of 'Medcroft Gardeners' will not be forgotten. But especially to my mother, Pat Moran, who taught me to read – and to love it! – thank you.

To my mother, Pat Moran,
and
in memory of my father, Frank Moran

Introduction

When my grandfather was a little boy, he was taken to see Queen Victoria when she visited Dublin in 1900. What excitement! As a towering mythic symbol, Victoria summed up an age and an ethos, a period spanning several generations, an empire that encircled the globe. On the day, however, my grandfather was sadly disillusioned. Instead of a commanding monarch, magnificent in crown, robes of state and sceptre, he glimpsed a tiny, stout figure in the carriage – a little serious and unbending, perhaps, but a woman who could have been anyone's widowed great-grandmother. My grandfather's experience seems an apt metaphor for the Victorian self-image. This was a society that simultaneously celebrated and disappointed itself, and that tension colours all aspects of Victorian culture, including its literary output. It also shapes how we understand that era today.

Queen Victoria's lengthy reign – from 1837 to 1901 – was shaped, at the start, by the legacy of radical **Romanticism*** and the Industrial Revolution and, at the end, by the possibilities of a new century. Representing a whole culture by the name of a single individual suggests it had a distinctive, uniform character; but it also signifies some of the core ideals of nineteenth-century Britain. Victorians valued stability, tradition, authority and grandeur in public life; so it is fitting that their culture is symbolically allied with the hereditary monarch, head of the most powerful nation of the day.

* Terms in bold indicate that they can be found in the Glossary, p.142.

Additionally, the strong identification with the Queen, who consciously portrayed herself as wife, mother and grieving widow, reminds us that Victorians imagined their society as a harmonious 'family', sustained by decency and sympathy, by duty and respect. Over a century later, we use the designation 'Victorian' to describe a period of literary and historical study – but also a complex culture. Like the double-exposure encapsulated in my grandfather's childhood memory, there is a gap between the period's self-projection as confident, accomplished and 'proper', and its untidy reality, marked by insecurity and doubt arising from vast social and intellectual change.

Of course, a distinctive cultural outlook does not suddenly begin and cease. Well before 1837, we can track ideas and events that seem characteristically 'Victorian', including, for example, an interest in social reform and the rights of the individual. The Victorian commitment to social improvement and democratization is anticipated in the 1829 Catholic Emancipation Act, which restored civil liberties to a significant minority, and in the 1832 Reform Act, which (modestly) extended the franchise. Similarly, the twentieth-century rebellion against Victorian artistic conventions and moral strictures was already well entrenched in certain avant-garde circles by the 1890s. Moreover, Victoria's reign was so long that it actually covered three generations, each with differing assumptions, worries and aspirations. Current scholarship employs loose but distinct subdivisions when defining the Victorian era: early, mid (or high) and late. While there are overlaps between these categories, each can be characterized by distinct attitudes. The Victorian period is a flexible framework marked by continuities, innovation and diversity.

'Early Victorian' culture, extending roughly to 1850, energetically embraced – even forced – changes, but, equally energetically, struggled to maintain a stable consensus about individual and communal purpose. Throughout this time of agitation and reform, fear of social unrest and economic instability appeared in public discourse and cultural products. An increasingly vocal working class, depressed markets, fierce competition and a significant influx of the foreign unemployed (including Irish immigrants) provoked concern about the condition of the country and the kinds of authority that should shape personal beliefs, social structure and behaviour. From the late 1830s, the prosperous middle class dominated this debate, enforcing *its* values as the means of satisfying both individual aspirations and the needs of the nation.

Between 1850 and the 1870s, 'high' or 'mid-Victorian' culture, with its devotion to the advancement of both individual and state, also evidenced the authoritative imprint of the middle class. Economic success and intellectual achievements, particularly those linked to industry, consolidated the power and status of the bourgeoisie. Middle-class devotion to individualism and a fervent Evangelical Christianity were systematically embedded in cultural practices, ranging from the 'natural' laws of free-market economics to guidebooks on self-help. Simultaneously, technological developments and social reforms improved the quality of life and supported a comforting sense of progress that benefited all. Yet, mid-Victorian controversies periodically undermined confidence. Unchecked urban expansion (creating problems of public health and crime), scientific developments (such as Darwin's theory of evolution) and scholarly research (like the historical analysis of religious texts) challenged orthodox convictions, both religious and secular.

The 'late Victorian' period inherited this contradictory mix of cultural assurance and self-doubt, but reimagined it as a battle between the outmoded values of the Victorian past and the rebellious, liberating possibilities of a more modern outlook. Of course, identity for many still depended on traditional moral and religious principles and codes of social conduct. However, a number of artists and intellectuals challenged the assumptions of previous generations, rejecting orthodox religious belief, mainstream models of gender and sexuality, and established artistic conventions. Instead, they reshaped the final years of Victoria's reign into a time of nervous but creative anticipation of a new century.

However, these trends are not the only continuities and discontinuities that permeate Victorian culture. Whatever the idealized rhetoric, no complex society is a single cohesive entity. Middle-class ideas certainly prevailed in the shaping of the country's self-image throughout the period. In public and private life – the sphere of the marketplace and the sphere of the home – aspirations and values reflect a bourgeois interpretation of experience. The importance of work, the individual's responsibility for self-improvement, the distinct and separate roles for men and women and the earnest commitment to duty commensurate with one's social place: these are just some of the middle-class principles that underpin Victorian social structures and artistic output. However, these viewpoints do need to be seen alongside the distinctive upper- and working-class cultures with which the middle class intersected – and competed.

Victorian literature was central to the struggle for cultural authority between different class-based value systems. Mainstream literary genres often implied a distinctively middle-class construction of social experience and individual identity. Novelists like Charles Dickens (1812–70) and Elizabeth Gaskell (1810–65) revealed the suffering of the underprivileged, but they indirectly downplayed the particular perspectives of the working class by promoting a romanticized vision of class collaboration and harmony. Their narratives typically allocate the heroic, active role to characters that demonstrate middle-class attitudes, whatever the apparent circumstances of their birth. As current literary scholarship indicates, these bourgeois perspectives masquerade as eternal truths in much Victorian writing and are embedded in the genres, narrative techniques and vocabulary of literary works, not simply in subject matter.

Although middle-class ideologies pervaded mainstream culture, their contradictions were uncomfortably apparent, even to Victorians. Nineteenth-century society firmly policed the boundaries of 'normal' identity with respect to gender and sexuality, nationhood, class and race. However, cultural differences were highly visible and often troubling. Unrest in the Empire suggested British civilization was not always welcomed as beneficial. Inflexible codes of respectability sat awkwardly with modern concepts of individualism and self-fulfilment. The conflict between personal self-expression and social orthodoxy, between autonomy and dutiful submission to authority, became increasingly difficult to resolve. Equally as hard to sustain was the popular Victorian image of a modern Britain with opportunities for the hard working. It was impossible to ignore the vast inequalities between those who had much and those who had nothing. Although the rhetoric of social mobility and progress implied merit would be rewarded, the reality was different. For many, the ideals of self-help and self-reliance translated into a constant stressful effort to escape, or at least retard, social decline in a brutal, competitive climate. Others worked the system with amoral gusto, sacrificing principles in order to 'get on'.

Aware of such tensions, we can no longer view the age as old-fashioned, conservative, or even simply repressed and hypocritical. Victorian culture, including its literature, was a dynamic, highly self-conscious and fiercely contested imagined space. New fields of knowledge, the great public institutions, personal belief systems and demanding social expectations presented both possibilities *and* drawbacks. As this book will go on to suggest, these hubs of power all advanced conflicting claims for an individual's attention and allegiance. All impacted on the ways Victorians saw and wrote about their world. The writer Henry James (1843–1916) once reflected on the difficulty of deciphering nineteenth-century novels, those 'loose, baggy monsters', as he termed them (1935: 84). In many ways, the story of Victorian literature and culture is also a narrative about interpretation – the struggle of a nation to give meaning and purpose to the loose, baggy monster that constituted its world.

1

Historical, Cultural and Intellectual Context

INTRODUCTION

Victorians recognized how much their identities and cultural products were shaped by the determining 'environment' (Pater [1893] 1896: 6). Such self-consciousness made the social milieu a favourite theme of Victorian writers. The novelist William Makepeace Thackeray (1811–63), for example, conveyed his sense of the era through historical context: 'we of a certain age belong to the new time and the old one. We are of the time of chivalry . . . We are of the age of steam' (1863: 110). Like many of his contemporaries, Thackeray saw his culture as one in transition, embracing the modern scientific revolution yet reluctant to surrender the values of the past.

The fields that constitute the Victorian historical, cultural and intellectual context – the arts, philosophy and religion, politics and economics, science and technology – provide a framework for understanding Victorian literature. Issues and trends in these areas are reflected in literary themes, genres and styles. They also account for attitudes about gender and sexuality, race and nationality, class and social structure that Victorian writers and readers often took for granted. For the modern scholar, context clarifies the codes Victorians employed when trying to interpret the social phenomena and developments of their age.

Contextual understanding reveals the assumptions that colour even the most 'factual' Victorian writing. Thomas Babington Macaulay's (1800–59) influential *History of England* (1849/1855), for example, is permeated by an unspoken view of progress that proclaims the triumph of the Victorian nation: 'the history of our country during the last hundred and sixty years is eminently the history of physical, of moral, and of intellectual improvement' ([1849] 1906: 10). By establishing continuity between the nation's past and its steady development, Macaulay reinforced confidence in the inherited religious, social and political systems of the period. Victorian imaginative writing is similarly laden with attitudes that many readers of the day shared, though often unconsciously. Contextualization helps a present-day reader understand the role of literature in reproducing or criticizing widely held values and beliefs.

It is important to think flexibly about Victorian cultural contexts. There is no single Victorian 'frame of mind' or 'grand narrative' that serves as a 'key' for decoding literary texts. The contexts we are about to consider reveal fluctuating priorities and tastes in response to historical changes of different kinds. Macaulay could optimistically see his environment as one of continued 'improvement'. However, a poet and critic of the next generation – Matthew Arnold (1822–88) – could perceive only an impoverished national spirit:

> these are damned times – everything is against one – . . . the spread of luxury, our physical enervation, the absence of great *natures*, the unavoidable contact with millions of small ones, newspapers, cities, light profligate friends . . . and the sickening consciousness of our difficulties. . . . (1996: 156)

As this observation demonstrates, nineteenth-century cultural contexts were sites of dialogue and opposition, rather than uniformity and consensus. Even contemporaries disagreed. Arnold mourned the intellectual and moral bankruptcy of his age, while the novelist Anthony Trollope (1815–82) felt his world 'less cruel, less violent, less selfish, less brutal' ([1883] 1974: 303–4).

The separation of contexts that follows – into the religious or political, for example – is something of an artificial device for organizing material. Throughout the period, the language and subject matter of different contexts intertwined in complex ways. A scientific topic might be presented through religious and political imagery, for example. Charles Kingsley (1819–75) argued that natural history developed 'that habit of mind which God . . . ordained for Englishmen', and was essential to 'the glorious work which God seems to have laid on the English race, to replenish the earth and subdue it' (1899: 308). While the topic is scientific, Kingsley's language actually promotes mainstream beliefs about what it is to be a 'normal' Victorian: energetic, knowledgeable and racially superior, with a mission to exert supremacy over the world. This mixture of discourses from different disciplines reinforces a particular view of nineteenth-century Englishness, while indicating that this identity is divinely sanctioned.

This example illustrates an important relationship between Victorian writing and Victorian culture. Victorian literature uses the rhetoric of many contexts to reflect and even redefine the culture of which it speaks. Art, politics, philosophy, religion, economics and science are all value-laden practices constituting the Victorian 'environment'. As an object of study, this cultural milieu incorporates multiple voices, competing for control over the shaping of knowledge, the interpretation of experience, and the formation of individual identities.

ARTS AND CULTURE: FORGING A NATION THROUGH TASTE

The public role of the arts

In Victorian society, the arts were viewed as an important sign of the nation's moral health and a vehicle for conveying social values. We can see this in the high visibility of the arts in the daily life of middle- and upper-class Victorians. Exhibitions were well attended. Trends in painting, literature and the theatre, as well as the pronouncements of artists, were widely discussed. Reviewers, academics, politicians, social commentators and members of the art community warred over subject matter, artistic style, changing tastes and the accessibility of the arts for new audiences.

From their immediate predecessors, early Victorians inherited a strong sense of the arts as a public institution defining national identity, whether this was through criticism or idealization. Cheap lithographs as well as expensive prints popularized work that had been influential in shaping British self-awareness, such as William Hogarth's eighteenth-century engravings (mocking the squalor and hypocrisy of contemporary London society), or the sublime, early nineteenth-century paintings of J. M. W. Turner (romanticizing the domestic landscape). Such seriousness was an expected component of art from the start of the period, evidenced in the taste for work in the 'grand style' – that is, formal, often large-scale, portrayals of classical, biblical and historical events, like Charles Eastlake's *Christ Blessing Little Children* (1839) and William Etty's *The Judgement of Paris* (1843). Yet early Victorians also set great store by sentimentality, catered for primarily in 'genre painting' – works featuring rustic, street and domestic scenes. Such touching examples as William Mulready's *Choosing the Wedding Gown* (1846) coupled charm with an obvious 'story' and simple, homespun lessons. In literary and visual work, moral weightiness and tender feelings were soon combined to instruct and move simultaneously. With its earnest tone, clear narrative line, contemporary settings, drama and pathos, Victorian art became a persuasive communicator of significant beliefs and values.

The role of art in conveying national values is exemplified by the work of Edwin Landseer, one of the best-known Victorian painters by mid-century. While his portraits of Queen Victoria and the Royal Family were popular for their sugared idealization of domestic devotion, Landseer was particularly renowned for his anthropomorphic depictions of animals with 'personalities', in situations that invited either laughter or tears (Treuherz 1993: 29). However, he introduced a new epic quality in his paintings of the rugged Highlands and beasts engaged in the battle for survival. His famous studies of Scottish deer, *The Stag at Bay* (1846) and *The Monarch of the Glen* (1851), are accomplished renderings of the wild animal but also defining images of a native character appropriate to an industrialized age. They speak of the nobility of the free, self-reliant individual; they depict the heroism of competitive struggle, even if it brings death.

The Victorian arts celebrated the nation, but also expressed concern about its new directions. When delineating the detail of contemporary social life, literary and visual works often created the impression that the modern world was both exciting and risky. Charles Dickens's novels, *Bleak House* (1852–3) and *Little Dorrit* (1855–7), and William Powell Frith's panoramic painting, *The Railway Station* (1862), are similar in their presentation of the diverse characters of the Victorian metropolis, intermingling with, and even preying on, each other. Social evils were another popular subject for art that professed a public purpose. Elizabeth Gaskell's novel, *Ruth* (1853), and Augustus Egg's three-painting sequence, *Past and Present* (1858), both commented on modern sexual morality, though the sympathetic portrayal of the fallen woman shocked their contemporaries. Exposure of topical problems remained a significant feature of the arts throughout the period, as illustrated by the studies of destitution in Luke Fildes's painting, *Applicants for Admission to a Casual Ward* (1874), and George Gissing's (1857–1903) novel, *The Nether World* (1889).

Victorian art history and criticism also engaged in social analysis. John Ruskin (1819–1900), the eminent critic, argued that art expressed a society's character and beliefs. In *The Stones of Venice* (1851–3), he suggested that artistic achievement was directly connected to the nation's ethical and spiritual health. Because Ruskin believed that art works conveyed cultural values, he was primarily concerned with their ideologies, even when discussing matters of form and technique, an approach typical of many Victorian reviewers of art and culture. Since only sound ideas would generate good art, the critic functioned as public custodian and promulgator of moral *and* artistic standards.

Promoting the arts and culture was viewed as a worthy enterprise that would educate the nation. Public spaces, including the Houses of Parliament (rebuilt after the fire of 1834), were decorated with uplifting murals by British artists. Wealthy industrialists and philanthropists in centres like Liverpool underwrote funding for museums and art galleries so the populace could learn about their cultural inheritance. Major public art exhibitions, such as those at the Royal Academy, were treated as important social events. Paintings were also routinely purchased for the nation. At all points, however, there was strict policing of subjects and style. From the scathing reviews of the Catholic content of Pre-Raphaelite paintings (Anon 1851: 8) to the outraged letter from 'A British Matron' to *The Times* (1885: 10) about paintings of nude females at the Summer Exhibition, a close watch was kept to ensure propriety and orthodox views were maintained.

The development of the National Gallery, under the direction of painter Charles Eastlake, is one of the most striking examples of the ideological role the Victorians accorded to the arts and culture. The Gallery was intended as a place of enlightenment for all classes. Its Trafalgar Square location, the generous opening hours and free admission ensured that its treasures were accessible to everyone, not just the privileged. There were, of course, problems with these open access arrangements. Some of the 3,000 visitors a day seemed to view the gallery as a haven from inclement weather and a place to consume snacks, while the 'effluvia of so many human bodies' was thought to damage the varnish on the paintings (Robertson 1978: 95). Nonetheless, public attitudes to the acquisition policy illustrate Victorian cultural politics at work. Eastlake's leadership was central to 'elevating and purifying popular taste', because the collection recorded Western art history and provided a repository of perfect images that would inspire the nation and its artists (Robertson 1978: 80–1). Certainly, the Trustees, including the Prime Minister, Robert Peel, regarded the Gallery as a powerful instrument for shaping and controlling cultural ideals.

The arts and culture as commodities

Victorian art had an additional value among those with a strong investment in material luxury as a sign of social standing. The purchase of art, like the acquisition of commodities of all kinds, became a status symbol for the increasingly prosperous middle class. Connoisseurship demonstrated a refined and educated sensibility that could appreciate the products of imagination as well as of machines. Rich industrialists and professional men could afford to buy art, even if they did not have a prestigious family lineage and an inherited collection. Largely eschewing the 'Old Masters' and grand style favoured in aristocratic circles, middle-class purchasers forged a distinctive 'modern' identity by patronizing the work of living British artists, including Frith, Landseer and the Pre-Raphaelites (Lambourne 1999: 28–9; Treuherz 1993: 82–3). Their accessible subjects appealed to the self-made man with patriotic interest in national history and legend, tender feelings aroused by idealized views of women, children, pets and home, and a commitment to duty, honour and respectability. To a middle-class Victorian, contemporary art could be entertaining, reassuring and thought-provoking in its record of a vibrant social world and picturesque landscapes.

With Victorian Britain's rise as a world manufacturing nation, the arts and culture were exploited to assist the cruder processes of making and selling. Some commercial strategies seemed at odds with the notion of art as a superior form of cultural expression. In 1886, for example, when A. and F. Pears purchased the copyright of Millais's painting *Bubbles* (1865–6), to create an advertising poster for soap, the art community was appalled (Lambourne 1999: 180). Yet the venture successfully established strong 'brand recognition' for the product. Even more indicative of the commodification of the Victorian arts and manufacturing crafts was the Great Exhibition of 1851. Promoted by Prince Albert and covering a 14-acre site in London's Hyde Park, the Exhibition brought together over 100,000 exhibits of the best inventions, designs and manufactured goods from every part of the globe, and particularly from the British Empire (Auerbach 1999: 9).

Spectacle was a central feature. The Exhibition was housed in the Crystal Palace, a specially designed building of glass and iron with an enormous vaulted roof that represented an amazing engineering feat in itself. Inside, the visitor could marvel at exotic fabrics and the stuffed elephant and howdah imported from India, wonder at the mock-up of a mediaeval court in Gothic style, purchase items like fine furniture, jewellery and ornaments, and, above all, be impressed by the supremacy of the host country. Raw materials from Britain and the Empire were exhibited, and their uses explained. Individual rooms were devoted to the most up-to-date technology, like photographic equipment, cigarette-making machines and microscopes. Over six million people visited the Exhibition, including one woman from Cornwall who was reputedly 100 years old (Auerbach 1999: 137, 148). Interest was stimulated by wide press coverage, and access facilitated by special trains that brought tourists from all parts of the British Isles to see it. Reduced-price 'shilling days' enabled working-class and country folk to share in this celebration of the nation's might and ingenuity. As a showcase for contemporary manufacturing culture, the Exhibition confirmed Britain as the world leader in trade, territorial expansion and advanced science and technology. Above all, the Exhibition made a deep impact on the mid-Victorian sensibility, encouraging patriotism, and associating the expansion of knowledge and the acquisition of material commodities with the excitement of a modern age.

New audiences

The Victorian enthusiasm for self-development through self-help stimulated new audiences for the arts and culture. Alongside existing educational centres like colleges, universities and fine art schools such as the Royal Academy, new institutions catered for those without the qualifications or wealth to enter the established centres. The National Art Training Schools of South Kensington instructed teachers in industrial and manufacturing design and craftsmanship. Throughout the country, adult education classes for working-class people, provided by the Mechanics' Institutes and other venues, offered 'amusement and information for the leisure hours of those who might otherwise have been exposed to the temptation of corrupt reading or bad company' (Newman [1873] 1964: 367).

One of the most important Victorian institutions to improve middle-class access to the arts and culture was the fee-based lending or 'circulating' library, epitomized by Mudie's Select Library, founded in 1842 by Charles Edward Mudie. Although a significant part of his stock was always dedicated to non-fiction, Mudie shrewdly exploited the keen interest of the public in the literary arts. He invested heavily in the latest novels and poetry, both 'popular' and high-brow. Membership was by subscription starting at one guinea a year (Griest 1970: 17), so that even students at the 'secular' University College London could afford to join. Between 1853 and 1862, Mudie increased his stock by over 950,000 volumes, and, in its heyday, his Library was said to have had over 50,000 subscribers (Griest 1970: 21, 79). Branches spread through London, and the firm shipped books to readers in the provinces and colonies. Mudie's success and the entry of other strong competitors into this field (such as W. H. Smith's) indicate not only the importance of reading as a Victorian leisure activity, but also the numbers eager to engage with a broad spectrum of contemporary writing, especially fiction.

Mudie's influence on the literary arts stemmed from the commercial pressure he exerted by ordering multiple copies of works. For example, he negotiated a bulk rate for a purchase of 3,100 copies of *Silas Marner* (1861) by George Eliot (1819–80) (Griest 1970: 87). Because subscription fees related to the number of volumes borrowed at a time, Mudie and publishers both had an interest in maintaining the expensive 'triple-decker', the standard three-volume format in which most novels of the period were first issued. Rather like the paperback trade today, cheap single-volume editions (suited, for example, to the new phenomenon of the railway journey) were usually delayed until some time after three-volume publication.

Mudie's phenomenal purchasing power served as an indirect mode of patronage and censorship. Books bought *en masse* and advertised heavily became 'bestsellers' automatically. Moreover, the Evangelical Mudie had stern views about the content of the books; indeed, his firm's title – a '*Select* Library' – implied high and 'proper' standards. Sharing his subscribers' notions of respectability, he banned or withdrew works deemed lewd or unseemly, like George Meredith's (1828–1909) *The Ordeal of Richard Feverel* (1859) with its plot about a wife who deserts her husband, and a marriage against parental wishes. Works were altered in draft to ensure they would not fall foul of his strictures. Anthony Trollope changed 'fat stomach' to 'deep chest' in his novel, *Barchester Towers* (1857), to avoid the kind of 'vulgarity' and 'exaggeration' that offended Mudie (Sutherland 1976: 27). The phenomenon of the circulating library is an excellent illustration of the way the new economics of Victorian mass-market publishing directly influenced artistic expression.

The arts, culture and victorian morality

Writers and visual artists who wanted to depict the gritty realities of contemporary life or challenge conventional attitudes
were constrained by the general tone of self-righteousness
that characterized middle-class culture. Some joked sardon-
ically about the overbearing presence of 'Mrs Grundy', a
character from an eighteenth-century play who objected to
almost everything. Yet the hypercritical watchfulness that
permeated both private circles and public life was discon-
certing and depressing. In 1851, William Johnston described
his age as one of apprehension: 'fear of the social circle, fear
of the newspaper, fear of being odd . . . still greater fear of
what somebody may say' (Houghton 1957: 398). To escape
seeming an improper influence, authors used coded, indirect
terms to express unorthodox attitudes, particularly in the
handling of romantic liaisons and sexual conduct, cross-class
relationships and Christian belief.

Numerous writers shared the loathing of heavy-handed
censoring mechanisms, like Mudie's library, expressed by
the novelist, George Moore (1852–1933), in *Literature at Nurse,
or, Circulating Morals* (1885). Nonetheless, most Victorians
believed the arts offered enlightenment of *some* kind. The critic
and poet, Matthew Arnold, for instance, saw an opportunity
for literature to replace Christianity as a source of spiritual
understanding. While religious institutions lost credibility,
Arnold believed that poetry would be able 'to interpret life for
us, to console us, to sustain us' ([1888] 1911: 2). Arnold's
influential theory established high culture as a bulwark against
the deadening vulgarity of middle-class [philistinism] and
moral prescription. Because culture encapsulated the 'best
which has been thought and said in the world', it had moral
weight and preserved universal values superior to any tempo-
rary preoccupation with appearances and manners
([1869]1966: 6).

While it is often said, in retrospect, that Victorian artistic
products are blinkered by prim moral and religious beliefs,
many critics of the day saw matters differently, at least until the

final decades of the period. Arnold, for instance, advocated the liberal arts as the antidote to the prudishness and anti-intellectualism of his society with its 'preference of doing to thinking' ([1869]1966: 129). The popular Victorian precepts of duty and work, of '*strictness of conscience*' and 'self-conquest', he termed 'Hebraism' (132). To this he contrasted 'Hellenism', showing the high respect Victorian intellectuals had for Greek classicism with its '*spontaneity of consciousness*' that informed culture (132). 'Sweetness and light' were Arnold's metaphors for the '*inward spiritual activity . . . increased life, increased sympathy*' that the arts stimulated when taken seriously and that, in turn, nourished 'the noble aspiration to leave the world better and happier than we found it' (64, 44). Because the arts would teach people to see truly, to discern hidden worth and to extend the reach of their sympathies, they would be central to the moral realignment of society.

Changing ideas about the nature and role of the arts

Even though Victorians relished debate about the role of the arts and culture, there was no consensus on the nature of the beautiful or the function of the artist. Tastes underwent dramatic change, as did assumptions about an artist's relation to society. In the eighteenth and early nineteenth centuries, the skill of the painter or writer depended on competence in handling a range of stylistic devices, and in choosing techniques and genres appropriate to the chosen subject. These standards were widely accepted and institutionalized through reviews, critical writing, universities and national bodies like the Royal Academy. As well as inheriting respect for these conventions, early Victorian taste was shaped by two traditions in both literature and fine arts: the remnants of Neo-Classical formality with its structural regularities and classical topics and allusions; and the rich language, emotive tone and sublime subjects characteristic of Romanticism. Because both modes explored such central themes as the role of creativity and imagination, the importance of freedom and the nature of personal heroism, the artist had significant status as the mediator of elevated truths and principles.

However, rapid social change, the challenges of everyday life in an industrial economy and new discoveries about the physical world gradually modified cultural tastes. By mid-century, the most admired works of visual and literary art seemed to engage directly with the 'real' world, largely through narrative forms. Embedded in a complex social milieu, the artist was expected to represent the immediate material environment and interpret its ramifications. John Ruskin, for example, urged painters to develop the analytical skills and knowledge of the scientist in order to convey the truth of the object portrayed, 'following the steps of nature and tracing the finger of God' (1903: 623). For the novelist George Eliot, the careful mirroring of 'real' social behaviour and thought processes in fiction was central to the artist's role as moral teacher. As she claims in *Adam Bede* (1859), the accurate representation of everyday experience enhances sympathy for 'the real breathing men and women, who can be cheered and helped onward by your fellow-feeling, your forbearance, your outspoken, brave justice' ([1859]1980: 178).

From the 1870s, new Continental artistic movements influenced Victorian ideas about the beautiful, the artist's relationship to society and the role of culture in shaping public values. French Naturalism, transposed to a British scene by such writers as George Moore, was controversial because it investigated social relations and aspects of experience previously excluded from mainstream fiction, while its emphasis on the powerlessness of individuals seemed devoid of any uplifting moral purpose. French Symbolism challenged Victorian assumptions through style as well as subject. It replaced the detailed descriptions and explicitness of realist writing with bizarre, evocative images defying easy interpretation. Symbolist art revelled in mood rather than moral precept. Together these movements threatened to make British arts and culture a foreign territory that rejected Victorian beliefs, and many reviewers and members of the public objected to them.

By the 1880s, the 'art for art's sake' movement – known as Aestheticism – had introduced a new relationship of the arts to society. Initially regarded as a cult adopted by 'advanced thinkers' and avant-garde cultural rebels, Aestheticism focused on the beautiful form of the work and its sensuous and emotional effects, rather than on moral content. When the Aesthetic essayist, Walter Pater (1839–94), claimed that poetry was 'all literary production which attains the power of giving pleasure by its form, as distinct from its matter' ([1873] 1893: 244), he deliberately broke with the moral didacticism, high seriousness and public role which early and mid-Victorians had allocated to the arts and culture.

Although traditionalists denounced the theories of Aestheticism, the movement had a major impact on form and design, especially in architecture and interior decoration. In the 1860s, the design company of the writer, socialist and Pre-Raphaelite artist, William Morris (1834–96), had anticipated Aesthetic principles by privileging form for its own sake; his firm's striking motifs for textiles, wallpaper and stained-glass windows flattened and stylized natural shapes. The Arts and Crafts movement of the 1880s further developed Morris's love of mediaeval simplicity and stylization. However, under the influence of Aestheticism, the European 'Art Nouveau' movement of the 1890s made even more of 'form', rather than content and 'meaning', as the central interest in decorative arts. Sinuous, undulating shapes, repeated geometric patterning and fantastic elaborations replaced simple representationalism, as seen in the illustrations of Walter Crane and the dissolute drawings of Aubrey Beardsley. By the end of the century, even the most respectable middle-class drawing-room incorporated some element of this distinctively 'modern' taste in the arts.

Popular trends in arts and culture

Tracking the gradual shift in Victorian ideas about art – from idealization through realism to a delight in beautiful form for its own sake – is to take a bird's-eye view. On the ground, as it were, most Victorians were more likely to engage with the arts through particular fads and fashions. Two were especially important for the shaping of the Victorian self-image: the taste for neo-mediaevalism and the Gothic, and the later passion for Orientalism.

The early and mid-Victorian delight in a fantasy recreation of the Middle Ages through the mimicry of visual and literary subjects and styles, clothing, architecture, interior design and ceremonials was evident in most Victorian cultural artefacts and practices: from church architecture and household furniture, to poetry and spectacular masquerade parties. The trend shows the Victorians were prone to define themselves by their cultural inheritance. From the 1840s through the 1860s, the Gothic Revival, stimulated by the architectural theories of Augustus Welby Pugin and the writings of John Ruskin, attempted to recover lost values through the imitation of past artistic forms. Pugin, for example, sought to reintroduce the Christian commitment of pre-Reformation England into Victorian society by reviving the architectural style of mediaeval churches. His Gothic decorations for the 1837 rebuilding of the (secular) Houses of Parliament illustrate how this fashion for mediaevalism expressed an idealized version of nationhood. The building's ornate detail aligned Victorian government with a romanticized British past, in which freedom replaced brutish feudalism and in which legislators were commanding, chivalric heroes. Alternatively, poets like Alfred Lord Tennyson (1809–92) and William Morris used the Middle Ages – particularly the legends of King Arthur – to comment on contemporary life. Tennyson's *Idylls of the King* (1859–85), for instance, suggested a number of parallels between the hopes and disasters of Camelot and Victorian ethical ideals and dilemmas. The poem remained upbeat in promising renewal from defeat, but suggested how easily virtues like duty, loyalty, love and self-discipline might be corrupted.

In the second half of the period, an interest in the Orient (in its broadest terms, non-Western cultures including the

Middle East and India as well as China and Japan) also influenced style and theme in the arts. The incorporation of Oriental designs and artefacts into furnishings, paintings, and even *The Mikado* (1885), a light opera by W. S. Gilbert (1836–1911) and Arthur Sullivan (1842–1900), signals curiosity about mysterious, foreign nations. However, as an artistic fashion, Orientalism promoted a particular view of the cultural Other. Representations of the Orient as a place of eroticism and primitive beliefs translated 'difference' as 'inferiority'. The absorption of Oriental details into Western art forms also implied the supremacy of Britain, which could reduce other cultures to exotic objects of inspection and exchange. When treated as luxury decorations, Oriental artefacts were silenced, becoming mere acquisitions rather than conduits of meaning in their own right. In the end, Orientalism offered reassurance about Victorian sovereignty rather than an open encounter with alternative viewpoints.

Popular culture

While these trends can be charted across the Victorian cultural scene as a whole, it is also possible to distinguish between cultural products in relation to the social groups that created and used them. What might be called 'high culture' intended for upper-class audiences – serious literature and theatre, the visual and plastic arts, quality newspapers, classical music – co-existed with more popular forms of entertainment associated largely with the working class. While many of these drew on contemporary middle-class preoccupations, such as patriotism and the marvels of modern science, they sometimes offered a sceptical interpretation of establishment authority, values and manners. Music hall performers, street entertainers and comic papers, for example, could rouse audiences with sentimental and jingoistic images, but they could also make light of the pretensions of 'toffs' and 'swells' in ribald ditties, skits and cartoons (Bailey 1998).

Many areas of popular culture that we would deem leisure activities – such as tourism, sport and reading – appealed to all classes, though not in a shared way. The working-class teetotaller might take one of Thomas Cook's recreational railway day trips for temperance groups, whereas the wealthy middle-class family would tour on the Continent. The middle-class reader who wanted to thrill to the secret crimes hidden behind the veneer of polite society might choose the sensation novels of Wilkie Collins (1824–89); the literate servant would find gore, shock and adventure in the luridly illustrated pulp narratives, called 'penny dreadfuls' and 'penny bloods' after their price and subject matter. Public spectacles, including balloon ascents, open-air concerts and puppet theatres, circuses and fairs, or venues like pleasure gardens, drew crowds from many walks of life. Certainly, middle-class Victorians all had some awareness of popular entertainment, as we can tell from literary work targeted at them. Charles Dickens regularly alluded to popular culture in his fiction and journalism, and exploited motifs and characters from them, as in *The Old Curiosity Shop* (1840–1) (Schlicke 1985: 87–103). Similarly, 1860s 'sensation fiction' drew on the topics, if not the rhetoric, of Victorian popular journalism that notoriously directed attention to the police cells, the divorce court and the lunatic asylum.

The blend between 'high' and 'popular' culture is just one indication of the many ways in which the Victorian arts provide both a mainstream and a shadow narrative of the period. Artists and writers produced positive images of their contemporary world, but also offered representations that pointedly revealed its failings and abuses. Creators and consumers of culture demanded high seriousness and moral probity, but also chafed against rigidity, righteousness and the policing of cultural and social boundaries. Whether enforcing or challenging artistic and social conventions, the arts and culture of Victorian Britain show us a society both confident and self-critical.

PHILOSOPHY AND RELIGION: CHALLENGING CERTAINTIES

Religion and Victorian society

One of the most successful novels of the age, *Robert Elsmere* (1888) by Mary (Mrs Humphry) Ward (1815–1920), was about a young clergyman's loss of faith (Sutherland 1989: 539). The popularity of this now obscure work reminds us that Christianity was *the* most powerful cultural presence in the Victorian milieu. Its beliefs and values shaped social behaviour through emphasis on duty, self-sacrifice and sexual propriety. It structured leisure time, defining in many house-holds what was read, said and done. Religious structures and terminology lie at the heart of the ideal Victorian family, with the *paterfamilias* as the patriarchal authority and the wife as the innocent 'angel' dedicated to his service. The Church offered professional career structures for men and, for women, a sense of purpose outside the home through phil-anthropic societies and projects.

The Protestant version of Christianity was a powerful cul-tural adhesive. The Anglican Church provided a spiritual power-base for the ruling class because it was the 'established' state church, regulated by Parliament and headed by the monarch. By displaying fervent religious commitment, the middle class legitimized its moral influence on the nation and the working class asserted its respectability and right to social inclusion. A Protestant foundation underpinned many charity and public schools as well as the great universities. Indeed, at Oxford, the required allegiance to the Anglican faith was not abolished until 1871 (Green 1974: 151). In the absence of state welfare, religious institutions helped care for the poor, and sought to reform the marginalized (as in the 'Magdalen' asylums for fallen women). Certainly, cant, hypocrisy and puritanical repression were also part of the religious context, as Charlotte Brontë (1816–55) suggested in *Jane Eyre* (1847) through the sadistic Reverend Brocklehurst and the frigid mis-sionary, St. John Rivers. But whatever the scepticism about an

individual's religious sincerity or the validity of particular doctrines, Victorians inhabited an environment framed and interpreted by religious ideas and systems.

Religion and the reading public

Victorian reading habits largely reflected this religious ethos.
It is claimed that 'sermons outsold novels' in the period
(Houghton 1957: 21). While this is probably an exaggeration,
religious works, such as the Bible and John Bunyan's *Pilgrim's
Progress* (1678/84), figured prominently among the books
in many Victorian homes (Cruse [1935] 1962: 17). Every
denomination could count on a large readership for inspirational tracts, collections of hymns and theological articles.
Even 'secular' periodicals, like *Punch*, published their fair
share of writing on religious issues and displayed their own
religious biases, anti-Catholicism being a favourite.

Writing for children frequently inculcated explicit religious principles, as in the cautionary tale of moral decline
by Frederic W. Farrar (1831–1903), *Eric, Or Little By Little*
(1858), and Charles Kingsley's fantasy, *The Water-Babies*
(1863). In such juvenile literature, Christian precepts
were entangled with respectable social customs and good
manners for the instruction of youthful readers; religious
belief was hard to separate from sound citizenship. Many
literary works for adults similarly endorsed Christian teaching. For instance, Charlotte Yonge's (1823–1901) popular
novel, *The Heir of Redclyffe* (1853), and the religious
lyrics of Christina Rossetti (1830–94) and Alice Meynell
(1847–1922) portrayed suffering as God's will and forgiveness as the way to eternal reward. Writers who avoided
explicitly religious themes often expressed a nominally
Christian ethos. Charles Dickens employed the rhetoric
of sin, judgement and forgiveness (Oulton 2003: 125,
133–5) in *A Christmas Carol* (1843), *David Copperfield*
(1849–50) and *Little Dorrit* (1855–7) in order to promote self-
discipline, compassion and honesty as the basis of social
justice. Dickens's representation of gender roles and

conduct, like the importance of female chastity, was also in keeping with Victorian Christian teaching.

Victorians who found religion painful or disquieting could turn to literature for reassurance. Historical novels about martyrs in the Early Christian Church, such as Charles Kingsley's *Hypatia* (1853) and Nicholas Wiseman's (1802–65) *Fabiola* (1854), encouraged religious perseverance. Combining gory sensations and spiritual inspiration in roughly equal measures, they disparaged nineteenth-century scepticism and greed by embedding these values in decadent 'pagan' cultures. Their lurid set pieces of heathen debauchery, sadistic torture and violent executions provided a chance to explore – and then condemn – erotic desires. The conversion novel, exemplified by John Henry Newman's (1801–90) *Loss and Gain* (1848), weighed up the profit and loss incurred by switching denominational allegiance or abandoning belief altogether. By showing converts' social dislocation and spiritual ecstasy, the genre reflected back to readers their own experience of the testing nature of faith in the nineteenth century. Later in the period, some authors presented doubt or disbelief as the 'modern' response to religion. James Thomson's (1832–82) poetic sequence, *The City of Dreadful Night* (1874), and Thomas Hardy's (1840–1928) last novels, including *Tess of the D'Urbervilles* (1891), provoked controversy by attacking religious hypocrisy head on, and questioning the Church as an authoritative vehicle of truth and social harmony.

Evangelicalism

Evangelicalism was the form of Protestantism that dominated religious thought. Associated in the eighteenth century with Nonconformist sects separate from the national (Anglican) Church, it taught that only faith could save sinners and that the Bible had absolute authority. In the Victorian period, most denominations evidenced some form of Evangelical enthusiasm, together with its characteristic emphasis on sin, reparation and personal salvation. The belief and worship of the Anglican 'Low Church' party had an Evangelical nuance, while the extrovert piety of new devotional practices in the Roman Catholic Church paralleled Evangelical fervour (Heimann 1995: 170).

Evangelicalism shaped the nineteenth-century cultural imagination. Emphasis on the fallen nature of humanity etched introspection and guilt on the Victorian personality. Self-awareness meant knowing one's wickedness and being constantly attuned to the dangers of temptation that lurked everywhere. Personal conversion was the balance to such unworthiness, and its importance influenced Victorian attitudes to behaviour in many ways. Because pious, 'proper' conduct was a visible sign of conversion and redemption, the evangelically-minded middle class judged *any* departure from expected standards as a sign of spiritual failing. This is why they distinguished harshly between the 'deserving' poor (gainfully employed, dutiful and righteous) and the 'undeserving' (unemployed, idle and morally suspect). 'Signs' of the convert's change of heart were eagerly sought, since they confirmed 'election' in spiritual and social senses of the word. The earnest Miss Clack, in Wilkie Collins's *The Moonstone* (1868), is a gentle caricature of the Evangelical enthusiast trying hard to save others by pushing uplifting tracts upon all and sundry. Evangelical conversion even provided the basis for the formulaic structure typical of Victorian autobiographical fiction and non-fiction: a crisis leads to self-loathing, contrition and a turning to new values.

Evangelical worship and teaching emphasized the emotional dimension of faith. For the average Victorian brought up in a family with Evangelical leanings, religion was 'a state of heart'; 'sudden, patent, palpable' feeling signified a sincere conversion (Gosse [1907] 1922: 180). Such attitudes encouraged the cultivation of the 'tender feelings' or 'moral sentiments' thought to inspire good conduct. For example, although the novelist George Eliot abandoned her Evangelical upbringing, she maintained that compassion and sympathy were central to social harmony. She wanted her readers to '*imagine* and to *feel* the pains and joys of those who

differ from themselves' (Eliot 1954: 111). The excess of sentimentality apparent in Victorian popular culture stemmed
from similar attitudes; it was not indulgence, but a desir-
able means of articulating 'shared moral feelings' (Kaplan
1987: 3).

The Anglican Broad Church

In addition to the 'Low Church' evangelicals, a Broad
Church party had emerged in the national Church by the
1850s. Favouring liberal theology over Evangelical dogmatism, Broad Churchmen, such as Thomas Arnold (of Rugby
School) and Benjamin Jowett (Master of Balliol College,
Oxford), took a moderate line on the Bible as an inspired
text, rejected 'superstitious' trappings like miracles and ceremonials, and highlighted God's generous forgiveness rather
than His punishment for sin. Broad Church theology encouraged Christians to act in, rather than reject, the world. F. D.
Maurice's Christian Socialism advocated social and educational reform to create 'an organic Christian Society' (Wolff
1977: 269). Broad Church 'Muscular Christianity' promoted
the healthy, active body as part of God's creation. Indeed,
such religious teaching was central to Victorian gender construction. In the writings of Charles Kingsley and in the
novel *Tom Brown's Schooldays* (1857), by Thomas Hughes
(1822–96), manliness is synonymous with a strong, assertive
and heterosexual male body that could work God's purpose
in the world.

The Anglican High Church and the Oxford Movement

Downplaying the Evangelical emphasis on private judgement for arriving at God's truth, the Anglican 'High Church'
wing focused on the Church's historical lineage and tradition, expressed through its ceremony, sacraments and rules.
In 1833, a group of prominent Oxford High Churchmen,
including John Keble, John Henry Newman and Edward
Bouverie Pusey, began publication of a series of reforming

Tracts for the Times (1833–41), and thus established the Oxford (or Tractarian) Movement. Wishing to free the Church from political interference, they argued that Anglican bishops inherited their power directly from Christ and His apostles, not from any monarch or parliament. Yet 'Apostolic Succession' inevitably associated the Church of England with its Early Christian, and hence Catholic, roots – an especially daring suggestion since Britain traced its constitutional freedoms to the Protestant Reformation. Castigated as misguided, if not heretical and dangerous, the Tractarians were further connected with a 'foreign' faith through 'Ritualist' followers who added elaborate Catholic ceremonial to Anglican worship. When John Henry Newman converted to Roman Catholicism in 1845, the nation was shocked, and Victorian cultural memory continued to bear the scars of this 'mistake' and 'misfortune', as Newman's decision was subsequently dubbed (Disraeli [1870] 1975: xiii).

Roman Catholicism

In Victorian culture, Roman Catholicism was the religious Other against which a healthy Protestant identity could be defined. Ideals of race, class, gender and nationality were reinforced through contrast to caricatured versions of Catholics as duplicitous, greedy, sexually abnormal, foreign in outlook and enslaved to the despotic Pope. Despite the Catholic Emancipation Act (1829) which had restored civil liberties to Catholics, they had difficulty integrating into mainstream culture. They had limited opportunities in professions like the military, could not attend Oxford or Cambridge, and were despised for their mysterious practices (like private confession), elaborate rituals and 'incredible' beliefs (like the transformation of bread and wine into the real body and blood of Christ in the Mass). Additionally, with its international network of missionaries, the Catholic Church rivalled the British Empire; and anti-Catholic propaganda suggested that it was only a matter of time before the old Roman enemy reasserted itself on British soil and destabilized the Victorian way of life. When the Pope re-established the Hierarchy of Bishops in England in 1850, many suspected this 'Papal Aggression' was an insolent Vatican plot to undermine the nation, especially when one new diocese was titled 'Westminster', the seat of Parliament.

Wounds were kept festering by the publication of Newman's eloquent autobiography, *Apologia pro Vita Sua* (1864), and by the steady leakage of Protestant converts to the Catholic faith, including the poet Gerard Manley Hopkins (1844–89). Protestants were dismayed as Catholic numbers grew rapidly, increased especially by the influx of Irish immigrants in the 1840s and 1850s. Despite the gradual move of Catholics into the establishment during the period, prejudices remained. The anti-Catholic sentiments of Robert Browning's (1812–89) 'Soliloquy of the Spanish Cloister' (1842) and Kingsley's *Westward Ho!* (1855) are still visible in Mary Ward's *Helbeck of Bannisdale* (1898), with its portrayal of a rigid Catholic.

The challenge to religious faith

Historical scholarship and scientific discoveries threatened the religious faith of many Victorians. By treating the Bible as an ancient document rather than God's revelation, the 'Higher Criticism' of French and German researchers challenged the accuracy of the Gospels and Christ's divinity. Sceptical 'biographies' of Christ, such as David Strauss's (1808–74) *The Life of Jesus* (1835–6), Ernest Renan's (1823–96) *Vie de Jésus* (1863) and John Seeley's *Ecce Homo* (1866), with their rational, evidence-based approach to Biblical history, seemed persuasive. When George Eliot translated Strauss's text in 1846, her doubts about the supernatural basis of Christianity were confirmed (Hodgson 2001: 6).

Advances in the natural sciences also undermined belief in the literal truth of the Bible. Geological discoveries suggested the earth predated any timeline that could be deduced from the Old Testament. Prehistory seemed a time of monsters and chaos, not the orderly creation of all species in six days. Charles Darwin's (1809–82) *On the Origin of Species by Means of Natural Selection* (1859) further eroded faith in God as Creator. Darwin's theories of adaptation and evolution suggested species developed gradually through chance and mechanistic natural laws, not by instantaneous Divine action.

Darwin's representation of natural history as a process of competition and 'survival of the fittest' cast doubt on God's Providential plan for humanity. As Darwin argued in *The Descent of Man* (1871), human beings were subject to the same evolutionary mechanisms as other species in terms of their origin from more primitive forms and their possible extinction. Such views were not entirely new. Tennyson's elegy, *In Memoriam* (1850), had incorporated similar fears, but Darwin's scientific approach seemed to provide tangible evidence for a non-religious interpretation of creation. *On the Origin of Species* kindled ferocious debate that set science and religion in opposition, hastened the advance of secularism as the dominant social framework, and influenced literary structures and themes.

Alternatives to orthodox faith

As religion gradually lost its authority, 'doubt' for some Victorians became a permanent spiritual state. The poet Arthur Hugh Clough (1819–61) suspended judgement and comment in an agnostic 'religion of silence' (Wolff 1977: 364), while others, such as Algernon Swinburne (1837–1909), openly flaunted disbelief. His 'Hymn to Proserpine' (1866) depicts Christ as a god of death and the rise of Christianity as a disaster for civilization. On the whole, however, atheism was a position kept quietly to oneself and one's closest friends, given the connection between religious orthodoxy and respectability in the period.

Some sustained hope in the supernatural and the afterlife by seizing on spiritualism and similar occult practices. Robert Browning satirized the famous medium, Daniel Dunglas Home, as a charlatan in 'Mr Sludge, "The Medium" ' (1864).

However, not even the proven existence of out-and-out fraudsters could dissuade many people from investing money and faith in the theatrics of table-rapping, séances, automatic writing and mesmerism to make contact with the 'other' side. Nor was this a fringe cult. Eminent members of the establishment and the scientific community, including Alfred Tennyson, John Ruskin, the politician, William Gladstone, and the psychiatrist, Sigmund Freud, supported the Society for Psychical Research, founded in 1882 for the scientific investigation of occult phenomena (Oppenheim 1985: 135, 245). The Society is important, not only for indicating Victorian preoccupation with the supernatural, but also for illustrating increasing Victorian confidence in scientific observation, measurement and physical data to interpret experience and the environment.

Trends in moral philosophy

With theories of the soul in doubt, theories of the mind gained importance as a means of understanding and guiding human behaviour. Moral and metaphysical philosophy drew on new theories of consciousness that suggested a connection between the body and the mind. Philosopher-psychologists, such as Alexander Bain, argued that the nerves, emotions and will were central to influencing ethical conduct. Building on these insights and on the eighteenth-century philosophy of Sentimentalism with its confidence in the morality of 'the heart' (Kaplan 1987: 16), Victorians sought ways of cultivating the higher feelings, especially benevolence, as the basis of right action in private and public life.

The Positivist theories of the French philosopher Auguste Comte also integrated science and feeling. Concluding that advanced societies used 'positive', scientific laws, rather than supernatural explanations, to establish truth, Comte proposed the science of social phenomena, coupled with altruism, as the stimulus for reform. Agnostic Victorians, such as John Stuart Mill (1806–73), George Eliot and George Henry Lewes (1817–78), appreciated Comte's 'Religion of

Humanity' because it promised that moral, political and physical evils could be eradicated by a rational and sympathetic application of the laws of social development. By substituting Comte's 'scientific-humanist' philosophy (Wernick 2001: 2) for supernatural revelations, Positivists hoped to secure the benevolent outcomes of Christian ethics, even as faith itself waned.

Philosophic Radicalism and Utilitarianism

Philosophic Radicalism sloughed off all traces of religion in favour of reason in order to remake the social body. Early Victorian progressives, including John Stuart Mill, argued that the logical way of reforming society was to maximize individual freedom, minimize intervention from privileged authorities (like government) and ensure communal harmony through the carrots and sticks of self-interest, curtailing some personal liberties in order to protect others, such as private property and physical well-being. This philosophy had significant appeal, informing politics, economics and ethics and providing an ideological basis for individual self-development and self-management.

Philosophic Radicalism was itself heavily indebted to the Utilitarianism of Jeremy Bentham (1748–1832). This rational philosophy, as pervasively influential as Evangelicalism in early Victorian Britain (Young [1953] 2002: 8), judged right and wrong by the pleasure and pain an act produced for the greatest number of individuals. Morality could be measured 'scientifically' by calibrating degrees of such pleasure and pain. 'Utility' guided the formation of laws in the same way. 'Good' sanctions were those useful for securing individuals' happiness. Religion was irrelevant, as were emotive appeals to innate human rights, which Bentham ridiculed as mere 'nonsense on stilts' (Atkinson 1905: 109). Taken to its logical extremes, Utilitarianism resulted in a blinkered addiction to facts and statistics and a cruel indifference to feeling and imagination, much as Charles Dickens satirized it in *Hard Times* (1854).

Even in the more humane version proposed by John Stuart Mill, Utilitarianism embedded distaste for government interference in the Victorian psyche, particularly in relation to social welfare and economics. For Bentham, any reforms had to be grounded in open inquiry, factual data gathering, reports, legislation and inspection, rather than political horse-trading (Hoppen 1998: 95). His approach to social engineering revolutionized government administration, leading to numerous commissions on such diverse topics as trade unions and public schools. At its best, Utilitarianism thus suggested social progress depended on close attention to the lived experience and fulfilment of citizens.

The Utilitarian emphasis on individual self-interest, freedom and happiness had its popular expression in the Victorian obsession with individualism, which effectively became a doctrine of secular 'faith'. Given the middle-class confidence in personal effort and initiative as the means to success, it is not surprising that individualism shaped the ways such Victorians interpreted their place in the universe. Even science, such as Darwin's concept of the 'survival of the fittest', was harnessed to the individualist cause, justifying the need for each person to enter the competitive fray, to adapt, seize opportunities, get on or go under. Guidebooks that offered practical advice on self-development became extremely popular. Samuel Smiles' (1812–1904) famous manual, *Self-Help* (1859), is perhaps the best exemplar, and its construction of self-sufficiency as social duty is also characteristic of the Victorian view of individualism. For Smiles, national progress and personal 'industry, energy, and uprightness' were related: 'civilization itself is but a question of personal improvement' (1859: 2). In this way, individualism efficiently contributed to national 'vigour' and prosperity.

Some social philosophers, such as Mill, were certainly aware of tension between the dual Victorian passions for individual fulfilment and for social harmony and collective progress. His treatise, *On Liberty* (1859), acknowledged the need to balance self-assertion 'within the limits imposed by the rights and interests of others' ([1859] 1991: 70). On the other hand, Mill felt that social conventions imposing uniformity of behaviour threatened individual development. Self-realization was an important principle in his argument for female equality in *The Subjection of Women* (1869).

The Woman Question

'The Woman Question' was how Victorians referred to the cultural upheaval that arose from women's changing expectations about their roles and possible destinies. In fact, the term says more about the patriarchal assumptions of the nineteenth century than it does about the 'question'. That women could be represented as an 'object' for dissection and analysis, and as a collective 'problem' for solution, demonstrates the way Victorian social structures and institutions tried to impose a single version of ideal femininity in the period, much at odds with women's own sense of their experience. In Victorian culture, women were idolized, protected and oppressed. The qualities of female innocence, purity and passivity that were routinely celebrated in written and visual culture and continuously reinforced through religious teaching, medical and psychological theories and the law, also 'justified' the exclusion of women from the institutions of power that shaped their futures.

At the centre of the bourgeois view of women was the philosophy of the separate spheres. In *Sesame and Lilies* (1865), Ruskin enthusiastically summarized this belief: women were best equipped for the private or domestic realm; and men were naturally suited to the active, aggressive and intellectual domains of public life, including commerce, government and the professions. In this gender ideology, biological difference, together with assumptions about the contrasting psychological make-up of women and men, fixed social expectations. Theories about women's bodies, innocence, emotional (rather than rational) temperament and maternal, self-sacrificing instincts underpinned the concept of the Victorian female presence as spiritually inspiring. Indeed, the favourite metaphor for womanhood was the 'Angel in the House', a phrase adopted from the poetic sequence of that name (1854–61) by Coventry Patmore (1823–96).

In practice, as Florence Nightingale's (1820–1910) unpublished essay 'Cassandra' (1852) suggested, this flattering characterization of the tender feminine nature shackled middle-class women intellectually and forced them to attend to 'every trifler more selfish than themselves' ([1852] 1928: 401). They were 'protectively' enclosed in the home and subordinated to senior male figures: father and brothers when single, husband once married. Even in this 'natural' environment women lacked rights. When the Matrimonial Causes Act of 1857 made divorce more easily obtainable, the burden of proof needed by a woman against her husband was more extensive than that required by the husband against his wife. In the event of separation, a mother had few rights over her children. As late as 1878, she would be assured of custody of children under ten only if there had been ' "aggravated assault" by the father' (Basch 1974: 22). Until 1870, a married woman had no legal claims over her earnings or inheritance acquired after marriage; she gained rights over property and money she possessed prior to marriage only in 1882. Women's bodies were policed through social instruments, ranging from clothing fashions to the ready acceptance of sexual double standards which punished women, but forgave men, for erotic experience outside marriage.

Women had few opportunities to enter public life. They were excluded from higher education until the last quarter of the century, and did not have the right to vote. While working-class women out of necessity supported their families by labouring alongside men in factories, in the field, in service, or struggling with piecework, social pressure restricted middle-class women to domestic, 'nurturing' employment, such as teaching and the hated governess work that Anne Brontë (1820–49) described in *Agnes Grey* (1847). It was mainly in the literary arts, including scholarly writing and editorships, that women's public achievement was acknowledged, partly because most women writers stuck to topics and genres deemed suitable to their sphere and expertise: the refined arts, the management of the home, love, courtship, marriage, family life and fidelity in the face of temptation. It was also because women's contribution in this field was undeniable. Eminent writers like George Eliot, Elizabeth Gaskell, Christina Rossetti and Elizabeth Barrett Browning (1806–61) demonstrated women's intellectual and artistic talents, while popular authors like Ellen (Mrs Henry) Wood (1814–87), Margaret Oliphant (1828–97) and Mary Elizabeth Braddon (1835–1915) proved that women could succeed in the commercialized literary marketplace. These accomplished writers, journalists, reviewers and periodical editors handled the *business* of literature, negotiating with contributors and dealing with backers.

As shadowy, dependent presences in a society organized to sustain masculine power, Victorian women were inevitably judged by the reflected status of their male superior. A disgraced brother or failed father or husband was a serious social and financial impediment, as the Hales realize in Gaskell's *North and South* (1854–5). As exemplars of innocence, Victorian women were also judged by their own reputations. In matters of sexual conduct and social customs particularly, deviation was not permitted. A middle-class woman who engaged in sexual activity outside marriage faced exclusion – from fiancé or from husband and children, from the parental home, from friends and polite society. A Victorian 'fallen' woman might sink slowly into prostitution as the only way to escape starvation, unless, like the speaker of Amy Levy's (1861–89) 'Magdalen' (1884), she was taken into one of the asylums set up to 'rescue' and 'reform' such outcasts. Even women who stepped outside social convention in ways that seem to us unremarkable – in dress, speech, interests, through living a single life or campaigning to enter male preserves like the voting booth or the university – could expect criticism. Ridicule was heaped upon them by men who caricatured them as mad, wicked, foolish or ungrateful and by female anti-feminists, like Eliza Lynn Linton (1822–98), who suggested their 'fast ways', 'want of high principle and absence of tender feeling' diminished women's cultural influence (1883: 5).

Despite disabling social structures, many Victorian women, especially middle-class women, were conspicuous achievers and inspired other women to struggle for greater freedoms. Even though the male establishment chafed at the large number of sad, 'redundant' spinsters who sought employment because they lacked husbands to care for (Greg 1862), women repeatedly proved they could succeed outside the domestic enclosure. Feminist organizations like the Langham Place Group formed by Barbara Bodichon, Bessie Rayner Parkes and the poet Adelaide Procter campaigned effectively to improve women's education and career prospects as doctors, clerks, bookkeepers, typists, hotel managers, telegraph operators, photographers, print compositors and shop assistants (Lacey 1986: 11–2; 258–67). Though women were not admitted to full degree courses in Britain until 1878 (at University College London), they showed their ability to take up advanced study at new female colleges established at Cambridge and Oxford from 1869. Formidable women exercised considerable public influence. The nurse, Florence Nightingale, the philosophic radical, Harriet Martineau (1802–76), and the travel writer and novelist, Amelia Edwards (1831–92), brought about the reform of medical services, the improved public understanding of politics and economics, and the professionalization of Egyptian archaeology respectively.

Philosophies of liberty, individualism and reform encouraged Victorian women to break out from a cultural position of weakness and function as free, responsible citizens by questioning and rejecting the gender ideologies imposed on them. Today, many of the achievements of these activists seem quite limited; but they also signify a remarkable revolution. By the end of the century, the image of the submissive 'child-woman' had been vanquished by a strong individual with a voice of her own.

POLITICS AND ECONOMICS: CONSENSUS AND CONFLICT

A volatile scene: political and economic divisions in early Victorian Britain

For most Victorians, the rhythms of social life seemed distinctly modern: exhilarating in their strangeness, but also stressful. While new economic and political theories promised tremendous possibilities, they also created intractable problems. In 1843, Thomas Carlyle (1795–1881) denounced the 'Gospel of Mammonism' because the fevered drive for profits, based on the 'laws-of-war, named "fair competition"', created 'mutual hostility' between classes ([1843] 1965: 148). The Victorian metropolis illustrated this divisiveness. Friedrich Engels observed that, in Manchester, working-class areas were 'sharply separated' from middle-class districts, concealing from the wealthy of 'weak nerves the misery and grime which form the complement of their wealth' ([1845] 1920: 45, 47). The factionalized political and economic organization of early Victorian culture is visible in this spatial layout.

The eighteenth-century Industrial Revolution transformed Britain from an agricultural to a manufacturing nation, with a corresponding increase in urban population. However, Victorian know-how drove this change forward with unprecedented speed. In 1801, 66 per cent of the population of England and Wales was rural; by 1891, that figure had dropped to 25.5 per cent (Hoppen 1998: 12). The middle classes in particular thrived in a market-driven urban society, dependent on the supply of goods and services. Advocating an economy unfettered by regulatory mechanisms and taxes, they occupied cultural space previously held by the aristocracy. The financial power of merchants, industrialists and attendant professionals like bankers and lawyers, endowed them with social and political weight. The Birmingham metal manufacturing family, the Chamberlains, exemplify Victorian industrialists who entered local and national politics in successive generations, securing power at the highest level, while pushing forward civic improvements.

Even though the upper class still dominated government circles, the financial clout of the middle class meant that the bourgeois outlook increasingly determined social and moral standards, fashionable manners and political and economic policies. Pivotal in Britain's material advance, the Victorian businessman and entrepreneur became the new hero in the narrative of the nation. However, his rise was paralleled by the emergence of the new industrial worker increasingly in conflict, rather than alliance, with employers. 'Horizontal' bonds of class replaced the notion of an organic social structure in which all functioned collaboratively. Interests of employers (or 'masters') and workers (or functional 'hands') seemed more likely to be resolved by a struggle for power than by consensus.

Politics, economics and the rise of the Victorian city

Economic factors altered the social geography of Victorian Britain. The 'supply-and-demand' cycle required an ever-larger market and a seemingly endless supply of 'hands' to service its needs. Urban centres provided both. In big metropolitan conurbations like London, as well as in the major factory towns, the population expanded at a remarkable rate as steam machinery increased the scale and speed of manufacturing. Cities absorbed displaced country labourers, the unemployed from small towns and villages, and Irish immigrants seeking to escape the potato famine (1845–9). With their fast-paced way of life, these crowded centres exuded a distinctively modern energy, focused on the creation of wealth.

However, there was a bleak underside, also closely connected to the economic system. Urban infrastructures quickly became inadequate. Roads were congested and filthy, depositories for horse-droppings and rubbish. Rivers were polluted by factory waste and human sewage. Overcrowding, dilapidated housing, inadequate drainage and water supplies, vermin, dirt and poor food characterized life in the working-class ghettos. Diseases, including cholera and tuberculosis, industrial injuries and work-related illnesses like emphysema were common. The competitive economy was subject to frequent fluctuations, from boom through stagnation to bust. This fluidity made workers' wages undependable, forcing many into lives of criminality and vice simply to survive. As a shirt-maker testified, 'it was the low price paid for my labour that drove me to prostitution' (Mayhew 1971: 150). With its elegant townhouses and squalid slums, the Victorian city was a tangible manifestation of the disparities that arose from the new age of industrial capital.

From a political point of view, the problem of poverty seemed insuperable. Early in the period, Lord Melbourne, the Prime Minister, reputedly quoted Walter Scott to Queen Victoria when she expressed concern: ' "Why do you bother the poor? Leave them alone!" ' (Cecil 1953: 88). Yet even Melbourne had conceded that, from the perspective of public spending, he did indeed need to 'bother' the poor. His English Poor Law Reform Act in 1834 cut back local parish relief for the indigent, tying assistance to the dreaded workhouse, with its punitive separation of the sexes and humiliating, prison-like regimes. *Oliver Twist* (1837–9) was Charles Dickens's attempt to expose the horrors of this particular policy, provoking Melbourne's petulant complaint that the book focused too much on 'workhouses and coffin makers and pickpockets . . . I don't like them in *reality*, and therefore I don't wish to see them represented' (Cecil 1953: 85–6). Yet they existed nonetheless, and as local authorities struggled to build workhouses and continued to dole out emergency benefits to the destitute, many died of starvation.

Poverty and inhuman conditions in workhouses, sweatshops, factories and mines stirred the national conscience, sensitized by campaigning novels like Fanny Trollope's (1780–1863) *The Life and Adventures of Michael Armstrong, the Factory Boy* (1839–40). However, these circumstances also generated fear. Economic depression in the 'Hungry Forties' brought the possibility of class conflict to the fore, especially as the disadvantaged workers gathered together in towns and cities seemed particularly prone to unrest. Well before 1848 and the Year of Revolutions on the Continent, W. Cooke Taylor was filled with 'anxiety and apprehension' when visiting Lancashire factory towns. The crowds seemed to express 'something portentous and fearful' (1842: 5).

Taylor termed these workers an 'aggregate of masses', illustrating how middle-class Victorians often saw the working class: anonymous, unknown but powerful and, possibly, sinister. The poor could retreat into slums as into 'some huge and intricate forest' with 'recesses in which every abomination may be practised' (Vaughan 1843: 225, 224). Their territory was a source of social contamination, with slum diseases providing yet another image of their danger. They threatened to spread dissatisfaction and degradation like typhus, 'a pestiferous moral exhalation dangerous to all other classes of society' (Miall 1849: 350). Middle-class Victorians could tolerate 'deserving' workers with gainful employment, a respectful attitude to the owners and institutions of capital, and a willingness to work hard to survive. However, they were increasingly disquieted by a working class that asserted its own, separate identity and seemed to resent existing economic and political structures.

Victorian political and moral economies

A *laissez-faire*, or non-interventionist, monetary system was at the heart of the class-based social structure. Government interference through taxes and tariffs was resisted; confidence was placed in free competition, private property and individual entrepreneurship. Aggressive economic practice in which only the 'fit' were expected to survive was grounded in the new science of political economy. Widely acclaimed for its rationality, political economy applied so-called 'natural' and historical laws of growth, decline and social behaviour to national and private-sector economic trends and policies. It advocated rigid adherence to the rule of supply and demand, despite the suffering of those who lost their jobs as markets stagnated or found their wages cut to meet increased competition. The ways in which different classes were understood and represented were derived from political economy, especially from its reliance on personal responsibility and effort. Because risk-taking, self-help, hard work and individual enterprise all served the demands of the marketplace, these qualities were incorporated into definitions of both the conscientious, patriotic worker and the successful industrialist and professional.

Not all Victorians were impressed by this capitalist model, however. As Carlyle complained, it threatened peaceful consensus because the ethic of 'Cash-payment . . . absolves and liquidates all engagements of man' ([1843] 1965: 148). Many cultural critics, including John Ruskin, worried that society at large seemed indifferent to the antagonism and injustice arising from these principles. Blind trust in political economy had created a secular 'religion' devoted to the worship of 'the "Goddess of Getting-on", or "Britannia of the Market"' (Ruskin 1905: 448). To the observant, this economic system created a seemingly inevitable conflict between self-interest and social responsibility.

Victorians used a variety of representational strategies to square this particular circle. For example, the concept of the 'gentleman' was actively promoted through education, religious teaching, the arts and even recreational activities like sport. As Pip learns in Dickens's *Great Expectations* (1860–1), there is a difference between the true gentleman at 'heart' and the pseudo-gentleman in 'manner'. Only the former embodies genteel values that prove to be unrelated to wealth. A 'real' gentleman, rich or poor, would demonstrate a sense of fair play, kindness to those less fortunate, respect to those in authority, self-sufficiency and earnest endeavour. Vaguely attached to a sense of personal improvement but essentially conservative in its allegiance to the existing social structure, the 'gentleman' archetype was a potent way of suggesting individual fulfilment was compatible with social obligations and that responsible, dignified behaviour could be expected of those without money and rank.

Explicit arguments on behalf of a *moral* economy in which social justice balanced wealth creation were another way of addressing these economic contradictions, as evidenced in James Anthony Froude's (1818–94) *The Nemesis of Faith* (1849). This novel attacked a predatory system in which the rich man snatched 'the spoils of others' labour . . . skilfully availing himself of their necessities' while shutting 'up his heart against their cries to him for help' ([1849] 1988: 47). More subtlety was employed – but to the same effect – in fiction that explored what Carlyle termed the 'Condition of England' ([1843] 1965: 7) (see Chapter 2). Writers such as Dickens, Elizabeth Gaskell and Benjamin Disraeli (1804–81) movingly described the suffering of the working poor in their fiction, while they quietly asserted the inherent decency of middle-class heroes and heroines. By appealing to readers' pity and sympathy, they put the case for reform on a personal as much as on a political footing.

Largely in response to increased publicity about the misery of the poor, some voluntarily provided philanthropic aid. Such action sought to improve working-class conditions, not by changing the political and economic system, but by recourse to more tenuous concepts of personal empathy and humane treatment. As John Ruskin argued, justice in the relations of 'master and operative' depended on 'such affection as one man *owes* to another' ([1860] 1862: 6). Paradoxically, however, Victorian theories of social welfare often shared the assumptions about self-help and the work ethic that underpinned political economy. The destitute – not social structures – were usually the focus for reform. As late as the 1890s, for example, William Booth, the founder of the Salvation Army, devised a paternalistic rescue plan for the benighted poor – not of Darkest Africa and the 'uncivilized' reaches of Empire but, ironically, of 'Darkest England'. It entailed 'creating in them habits of industry, honesty, and truth' and 'exporting' them to the colonies 'so laying the foundations, perchance, of another Empire' (1890: 93).

Victorian politics at home

Party politics in the period was a decidedly complex affair. Prior to Victoria's reign, Parliament had been effectively a closed shop for the ruling classes. The First Reform Act (1832), which modestly increased the electorate, meant politicians now needed to win voters' support, though without making promises that would damage the economic and social status quo. Throughout the period, therefore, political parties reorganized to differentiate themselves more clearly from opponents and to enhance their appeal to the electorate. Consolidation of party interests along class lines is one narrative of Victorian politics: the unification of the (progressive) Whigs and (reforming) Radicals in the middle-class Liberal party dominated by Gladstone; the emergence of modern Conservatism led by Disraeli, whose patriotic support of traditional institutions and monarchy appealed particularly to the landed gentry and aristocracy; and the formation of the Labour Party under Keir Hardie at the turn of the century. Yet these party alignments are only one dimension of a fraught and fast-moving political scene, characterized by disruption and agitation and often driven by public anxiety and dissatisfaction.

Law-breaking and vice were subjects of continued concern which politicians were expected to address. Various measures were attempted. Middle-class neighbourhoods were gated to prevent the intrusion of unwelcome vagrants and criminals (Wilson 2002: 383). The Metropolitan Police Force, established by Robert Peel in 1829, concentrated on restraining the urban working class and ensuring that prostitutes, thieves and 'roughs' did not disturb public order. However, this heavy-handed approach increased resentment towards the establishment and the politicians; 'bobbies' or 'peelers' encroached on the personal freedom of the poor in ways that only exacerbated social tensions. Evidence of middle-class corruption added to public disquiet, undermining confidence in the innate respectability of the bourgeoisie. Its visibility in popular 'sensation fiction' by Wilkie Collins,

Charles Reade (1814–84) and Mary Elizabeth Braddon in the 1860s (see Chapter 2) reinforced a sense of the fragility of a society riven by individual greed, ambition and gullibility.

Activist campaigning, such as agitation for political empowerment through democratic reform, was a further reminder of social divisions. For example, the Chartist Movement, incorporating a variety of workers' groups, published a 'People's Charter' in 1838. It advocated such measures as the secret ballot and universal male suffrage. As the future Conservative Prime Minister, Benjamin Disraeli, suggested in his novel, *Sybil* (1845), Chartism stemmed directly from the economic divisions between the rich and the poor who formed '[t]wo nations; between whom there is no intercourse and no sympathy' and who were demonstrably 'not governed by the same laws' ([1845] 1920: 76). Charles Kingsley's *Alton Locke* (1850) depicted many Chartists as peaceful; but the movement was associated in the public mind with radical extremism. The high profile of their campaigns, including a petition to parliament with over one million signatures, the aggressive rhetoric of their songs and propaganda pamphlets and their support for strikes and (by some) more violent action, convinced many that the Chartists intended to destroy the social fabric in the name of political freedom. Lord Macaulay, for example, judged their desired reforms to be 'incompatible with property, and . . . consequently incompatible with civilization' (1880: 183). Although Chartism itself collapsed by the late 1840s, outbreaks of unrest continued, including the Hyde Park riots of 1866 (when over 200,000 electoral reform supporters agitated for the right of mass assembly) and the 1887 'Bloody Sunday' Trafalgar Square riots against unemployment (Newsome 1998: 48). Such public disorder ensured that conflict as much as consensus remained an ever-present possibility in a society 'of Money and of Hunger', of 'Drudges' and 'Dandies' (Carlyle [1833–4] 1937: 286).

Politicians responded to campaigns seeking improvement in virtually every cultural domain – from public health to electoral reform, from employment conditions to family law, from vivisection to education. The Second Reform Act (1867), on which George Eliot's *Felix Holt, The Radical* (1866) indirectly comments, enfranchized all men renting or owning property valued at over £10 (that is, virtually all male urban-dwellers). The Married Women's Property Acts of 1870 and 1882 gave women control over their assets and earnings. Before this, the plots of many novels had turned on the marriage of convenience and the plight of women pursued and abused by fortune-hunters, ranging from Anthony Trollope's *The Newcomes* (1853–5), to Wilkie Collins's *The Woman in White* (1859–60) and Dinah Mulock Craik's (1826–87) *A Noble Life* (1866). The Education Act of 1870 set up school districts and encouraged the building of primary schools. Education up to the age of 10 was made compulsory in 1880 and free in 1891. The Public Health Acts of 1848, 1872 and 1875 improved urban conditions by ensuring state oversight of fresh water supplies, drainage and sewage disposal. As mundane as sanitation reform might seem, it was an important signal that government accepted responsibility for the well-being of all citizens.

While these laws might give the impression that the ethos of Victorian politics was one of pro-active reform, many legislative changes were as much about compromise as permissiveness. Control through conciliation is apparent, for example, in the abolition of the protectionist Corn Laws (1846). While the Laws harmed the poor by keeping bread prices artificially high, their repeal mainly appeased middle-class employers who favoured all-out competition in an unregulated marketplace. Another example is the slow progress made on the extension of the franchise and electoral redistribution. The first Reform Act of 1832 was intended to quell unrest among the majority of the country (who had no voting rights) by reorganizing constituencies more fairly and modestly increasing the electorate, a benefit primarily for the middle class. Subsequent electoral acts did spread democratic participation but continued to exclude women, implying they might not be relied upon to preserve the (patriarchal) status quo.

A similar effect can be seen in laws pertaining to sexual conduct. By the 1880s, public sex scandals (ranging from homosexual brothels to evidence of sex traffic in young girls) had heightened panic about declining moral standards. Law – like medicine – was therefore brought to bear on the 'normalizing' and strict policing of sexual orthodoxy. The Labouchere Amendment to the Criminal Law Amendment Act of 1885 reconfigured the cultural understanding of homosexuality by focusing on male same-sex practices (rather than on particular sexual acts per se) and broadening definitions of criminal 'gross indecency' involving men. Erotic preference and sexual identity, rather than actions, now became the object of investigation and punishment. As a result, writers exercised even greater care in representing unconventional sexualities, and the public scrutinized work with even greater suspicion. For example, one reviewer condemned Oscar Wilde's (1854–1900) *The Picture of Dorian Gray* (1890/1) for its inclusion of 'matters only fitted for the Criminal Investigation Department' ([1890/1] 2005: xviii). When the new Act was invoked in 1895 to prosecute Wilde for homosexual practice, it was clear that politicized mechanisms would be imposed to control 'unruly' private desires.

Labour relations

The theory of political economy suggested that the risky battles of the marketplace were both an ennobling test of character and the inevitable cost of personal and national progress. The same ideas indicated 'labour' was the naturally ordained state of the working classes and their route to advancement and satisfaction. In 1834, Commissioners inquiring into the Poor Laws concluded labourers' contentment 'increased with their industry' (Young and Handcock 1956: 700). A factory inspector took exactly the same line in 1852, asserting both adult and child workers 'never were so well off' since they had employment, cheap food, clothing and entertainment, and 'time for some mental improvement' (Young and Handcock 1956: 992). The economic *realities*

for wage-earners proved otherwise. Brutal tactics were employed to increase profits and cut costs, including wage
reductions, excessive working hours, harsh penalties for
recalcitrance and the use of strike-breakers. Some employers
took the interests of the work force seriously and improved
housing, wages and conditions; yet there were many more
who exploited their employees and stifled dissent, blocking
co-operative support groups and trade unions.

The opposition of 'master' and 'men' became a familiar
antagonism, embodied not only in novels like Gaskell's *Mary
Barton* (1848), but also in the language of heavyweight economic analyses, government reports and popular essays.
From 1850, English readers could consult a translation of
The Communist Manifesto with its exhortation to all workers to
unite because they 'have nothing to lose but their chains'
(Marx and Engels [1848] 1930: 68), but on the whole,
English trade unions tended to be unrevolutionary, local
groups, established to protect wages. Nonetheless, they
were objects of much middle-class suspicion. Because they
challenged preconceptions about the natural justice of
private ownership and the balance of industrial and economic power, they were felt to foster 'a spirit of antagonism'
and to interfere with the comforting stereotype of the sturdy,
self-reliant and respectful British workman, as a Royal
Commission suggested in 1869:

> The desire of the workman to excel, to do the best in his power
> to give satisfaction to his employer, to improve himself, and if
> possible to rise in the world, is damped by the thraldom in
> which he is held to the rules of his union. (Young and Handcock
> 1956: 1005)

The union 'persecution' of workers who did not wish to join
– the central narrative impetus of Charles Reade's novel, *Put
Yourself in His Place* (1870) – also made the public mistrust
employee groups. The London Dock Strike of 1889 in a
sense realized middle-class fears; it illustrated just how much
force could be exerted by co-ordinated working-class action

to improve conditions and pay. The formation of the Fabian Society in 1884, the Socialist League in 1885 (led by William Morris) and the Independent Labour Party in 1893 marked the institutionalization of a distinctively working-class voice in the formal political spectrum of Victorian life. From this point, the conflict between classes deepened into a struggle over the social principles that should shape Britain's transition to a new century.

Ireland

The Irish Question factionalized Victorian political parties and plagued Prime Ministers who tried various tactics to pacify and subdue a community divided by religious, economic, political and cultural differences. The majority Catholic population in Ireland resented their poverty, limited opportunities and rule by a distant, Protestant colonizer – Westminster. They bitterly eyed the prosperity of the local Protestant establishment or 'ascendancy' (even though that was in fact waning throughout the nineteenth century). Such discontent raised the threat of rebellion that could spread to mainland Britain. The government attempted some conciliatory measures, such as modest financial relief to sufferers during the Irish potato famine of 1845–9. However, the public had scant sympathy. The destitute Irish who came to Britain in the wake of the famine simply reinforced a sense of Ireland as a land of wretched troublemakers. Seeking jobs at a time of economic depression on the mainland, when even the British workforce was hard pressed to find employment, they were reduced to begging and stealing, or were socially isolated in the most menial jobs and the most degrading slums.

By the 1880s, a political solution to the campaign for Irish independence was urgent. Irish nationalists used many strategies to force the hand of the British Government, as suggested in Trollope's unfinished novel *The Landleaguers* (1882–3). Civil action, including rent strikes and harvest boycotts, escalated to assassinations in Ireland and bombings on the mainland, including London, Salford and Glasgow. Prime Minister Gladstone favoured the Home Rule project of the Irish politician, Charles Parnell. It satisfied the Irish desire for self-government by granting the country its own parliament; but it gave Westminster continued control over Irish defence, foreign affairs, trade and customs and excise. Ultimately, political consensus on Ireland proved impossible to achieve. In fact, Irish nationalism disrupted British political stability by splitting the Liberal Party in 1886, and bringing it to defeat at the polls. Public opinion, though divided, in the main turned its face against Irish political and electoral reform. Bent on retaining, not sharing, power, Victorians were by and large prepared to sacrifice Irish freedom for the appearance of national cohesion.

Victorian politics abroad

Victorian Britain proclaimed its right to oversee world affairs. Patriotic fervour, visible in the cartoons and songs of popular culture and in establishment rhetoric, was just one way of asserting this authoritative global presence. A combative foreign policy also helped to secure Britain's international dominance and grip on foreign markets and raw materials, notwithstanding the territorial ambitions of the German Empire and Russia. British politicians were not averse to meddling – or threatening to meddle – in the internal affairs of foreign countries on the grounds of supporting freedom, while actually protecting British interests, as in the wars with China over the profitable opium trade.

However, the Crimean War (1854–6) had an ambivalent impact on the public perception of foreign policy. Hoping to curb Russian expansion, Britain joined France to support Turkey in her war with Russia. The Anglo-French campaign in the Bosphorous was technically successful, but devastating in terms of its operation: tactically ill-prepared, poorly equipped and badly led (one British general, a veteran of Waterloo, habitually referred to the French allies as 'the enemy') (Wilson 2002: 179). Many more British troops died from disease, especially cholera, than were killed in battle. Strategy was recklessly conceived and poorly executed. Tennyson's poem, 'The Charge of the Light Brigade' (1855), immortalized an act of valour during the Battle of Balaclava; but in reality it resulted from muddle and misjudgement on the part of the officers.

Public response to the War was mixed. The defeat of Russia and the incidents of daring against the odds bolstered Britain's self-image as the international scourge of tyranny. But the war was also the first campaign abroad to be covered by specialist correspondents, notably William Howard Russell of *The Times*. His impressions of horrific battles and the grisly conditions, which he telegraphed home, aroused considerable disenchantment with the military command responsible for needless illness, suffering and death. On one front only did the war really push culture forward. By generating favourable publicity for the nursing practices of Florence Nightingale, it furthered her campaign to professionalize nursing care and reform the Army Medical Service.

Empire

Modern historians are divided about the extent to which the average Victorian working-class man or woman knew and cared about the details of the imperial project, although postcolonial critics have shown how it permeated Victorian literature from Brontë's *Jane Eyre* (1847) to the work of Rudyard Kipling (1865–1936), H. G. Wells (1866–1946) and Joseph Conrad (1856–1924) at the turn of the century. Certainly, patriotic rhetoric was upbeat about British 'ownership' of vast regions, like Canada, Australia and New Zealand, and of enormous populations, like those of India. Victorian maps, dominated by the colour pink signifying British territorial holdings, also provided visible confirmation of power because the Empire demonstrably encircled the globe. When in 1876 Disraeli announced Queen Victoria would be known as 'Empress of India', he flattered the monarch but also reinforced the average Victorian's sense of

British supremacy. News of the unusual sights, peoples and customs across the Empire filled the columns of newspapers and magazines, stimulating curiosity about other cultures and encouraging the growth of human and social sciences like anthropology. There were career opportunities for all classes in colonial administration, imperial building and engineering schemes, importing and exporting businesses and in the army and navy that kept order on land and sea. Emigration to distant colonies offered many families chances for property and wealth that were beyond their grasp in Britain. Empire seemed to benefit everyone. As the journalist and explorer Henry Stanley cheerfully reminded a Chamber of Commerce meeting, industry profited from the manufacture of 'trinkets that shall adorn those dusky bosoms'; God and the colonized profited from missionaries' efforts 'to bring them, the poor benighted heathen, into the Christian fold' (Newsome 1998: 136). Today, it is apparent that such discourse concealed racial prejudice, economic exploitation and the erosion of other cultures by the forced implantation of British religion, education and law.

The peace that Empire 'guaranteed' existed more in the cultural imagination than in fact. In 1857 Indian soldiers rebelled against British commanders when particular orders insulted their religious beliefs. The atrocities perpetrated during the year-long Indian Mutiny drove home the fragility of Imperial rule. As a result, Whitehall tightened its grip on colonial governance, seizing control of India from the private East India Company, a huge trading organization that had previously run the country. From the 1860s national uprisings, wars and disputes in regions as diverse as New Zealand, Western Canada, West Africa and Malaya continued to test Britain's political will and military prowess. Increasingly, the imperial experience was connected with bloodshed, high expenditure and the growing restlessness of the colonized who often experienced Empire as alienating, degrading and oppressive. The power of these resentful and mysterious subjects became a source of anxiety as the period drew to a close. 'Reverse colonization', the destruction of the mother culture by the dangerous and intrusive immigrant, became a popular theme in fantasy novels of the 1890s, including Bram Stoker's (1847–1912) *Dracula* (1897) and Richard Marsh's (1857–1915) *The Beetle* (1897).

The 1899–1902 Boer War in South Africa ignominiously reversed the magic of imperial adventure, previously epitomized in novels like H. Rider Haggard's (1856–1925) *King Solomon's Mines* (1885) and in the real-life gold and diamond mining exploits of Cecil Rhodes. The campaign against the Dutch-descended Boers for possession of the Orange Free State and the Transvaal was technically successful, and Britain gained supremacy over a unified South Africa. But what lay beneath the bravado and celebrations at home in 1902 was a new vision of Empire captured in photographs and the accounts of volunteer relief workers: the ruthless General Kitchener's concentration camps, populated by starving and dying Boer women and children; a scorched earth devoid of crops and livestock; and extensive casualties on both sides (Judd and Surridge 2002: 187–96). Even under the consensus of patriotism, by the turn of the century serious moral fissures were undeniably apparent in the management of colonization and the expansion of Empire.

The mixed experience of imperialism – optimism and opportunity on the one hand, brutality and conflict on the other – is replicated throughout the Victorian cultural milieu. Politically, the period gave new opportunities to the ordinary individual. Reforms, including the introduction of the secret ballot and the extended franchise, more permissive legislation on property rights and family relationships, and improvements in public health and education, show a significant attention to the interests of the common people as well as to the ruling elite. By the time of Victoria's death, even the working classes could feel that they had a greater stake in the making of the nation. Yet the turn of the century could not really be faced with equanimity. Squalor and dehumanization were as apparent in 'darkest England' as in the far reaches of Empire. Participation in political and economic processes was still blocked for large sections of the community, including women. Those who moved too far outside cultural borderlines, or who argued for more radical freedoms, were unlikely to flourish. Dilemmas and friction seemed the dominant Victorian legacy to a new century.

DEVELOPMENTS IN SCIENCE AND TECHNOLOGY: THE KNOWLEDGE REVOLUTION

The democratization of science

In 1850, Queen Victoria's husband, Prince Albert, made a speech extolling the virtues of science and technology. By discovering 'the laws by which the Almighty governs His creation' and using these 'to conquer nature', scientists discharged 'a sacred mission' as 'divine instrument' (Albert 1862: 111–2). Considered in hindsight, this part of Albert's message was somewhat askew since Victorian scientific discoveries gradually eroded confidence in 'the Almighty'. Yet the Prince *did* put his finger on a very important feature of nineteenth-century science: its widespread dissemination and use. Understanding of the universe was no longer restricted to a privileged few. Even though the pace and volume of discovery made specialization inevitable, new scientific insights became 'the property of the community at large' (111).

Technological advances changed industry, stimulating the search for new products to consume as well as new means of manufacturing them quickly, cheaply and in volume for a mass market. But the 'community at large' experienced the knowledge revolution more directly. Scarcely a single aspect of daily life was untouched by science and technology. New modes of transportation, especially the railway, altered the relation of town and country, created a tourist industry, introduced ordinary people to their heritage and geography. Innovations in medicine changed forever the experience of illness, pain and death; inventions like the telegraph transformed communications; and safety was improved by such developments as electric street lighting from 1878. The human and social sciences provided insight into individual behaviour and the social environment. Even leisure activities, like photography and magic lantern 'slide shows', depended on the application of optics, chemistry and physics.

The 'democratization' of scientific knowledge also shaped the Victorian imagination, arousing intense curiosity about the material world and its workings. Scientific lectures and demonstrations and popular science articles in mass-market publications reached a significant portion of the community. The discourse of science inflected language and literature. A detailed attention to 'data' and 'facts' in part explains the Victorian love of history, biography and elaborate material details in fiction. Indeed, the very precision of scientific language implied a mastery of matter and thus the potential to regulate every aspect of experience. As the Darwinian biologist and science educator, Thomas H. Huxley, predicted, knowledge of the physical conditions of the universe 'may, in future, help us to exercise the same kind of control over the world of thought, as we already possess in respect of the material world' (1893: 164).

The professionalization of the sciences

New discoveries revolutionized the way the scientific community defined and practised its own disciplines. The professionalization of the sciences was a major phenomenon, evidenced not only in the growth of specialized fields, but also in the development of high-level training programmes and career paths on a par with traditional academic fields such as classics and philosophy. By the 1860s, major public schools, including Rugby and Harrow, incorporated scientific studies in the curriculum, and students could take Natural Sciences at Cambridge. Technological research was pursued in universities, and important academic links were made with major industrial firms (Hoppen 1998: 308–9). Overall, increased authority was vested in science as a cultural discourse.

Sciences of origin and human development

The Victorian discovery of mechanical and natural laws that accounted for the operations of matter profoundly altered intellectual life. Charles Lyell's *Principles of Geology* (1830–33) and Robert Chambers's *Vestiges of the Natural History of Creation* (1844) posed new questions about the origins and age of the Earth and the laws by which it evolved. Evidence of fossil remains and of slow natural processes like erosion suggested a lengthy historical process in which God's role was indistinct. Through biology and natural history, Charles Darwin filled out this account of creation as a mechanical operation dependent on a mixture of fixed laws and chance.

As a naturalist on a survey ship in 1831, Darwin had made a detailed study of geological features and flora and fauna in such places as the Galapagos Islands, establishing how particular organisms had 'mutated' in response to different environments and passed on their 'alterations' to subsequent generations. Postulating that new species slowly emerged from this process of adaptation and survival, Darwin developed the hypothesis of evolution through natural selection, published in *On the Origin of Species* (1859). His theories both confirmed and challenged core Victorian ideals. For optimists, they seemed to prove the inevitability of society's progress through adaptation to new conditions. However, others thought Darwinism replaced the Biblical narrative of divine creation with a sterile record of blind, amoral processes and a brute struggle for survival. Humanity was no longer the apex of God's creative energy but an animal species derived 'naturally' from lower animal types and subject to extinction like any other genus.

Once science began to formulate a view of human life shaped – like that of animals – by chance, heredity and accidents of birth, confidence in willed decision-making and personal responsibility was significantly diminished. Such theories influenced literature, not only in theme but also in style. From the 1860s onwards, novel plots began to reflect the determinism of a Darwinian universe. Characters ceased to be controlling agents, learning from experience and shaping their own destinies. Instead, like the protagonists of Hardy's *The Mayor of Casterbridge* (1886) and *Tess of the D'Urbervilles* (1891), they became the tragic victims of both natural and social laws.

Sciences of the body and mind

The knowledge revolution affected attitudes to the body. Notwithstanding the many anecdotes about the Victorian propensity for hiding bodily parts, the understanding and improvement of the physical self were matters of great interest. Science promised ways of exerting control over the body's wayward desires and perfecting its potential to the benefit of individual and society at large. For men, this meant improving physical energy and stamina in order to take up the challenges of public life; for women, it entailed preserving health, especially sexual health, to fulfil their childbearing role. Better understanding of the mechanics of the body drew science into the discourses of many fields, ranging from sport to religion.

Advances in medicine encouraged a more 'optimistic' approach to bodily experience. In 1854, the doctor John Snow offered evidence that the ravaging disease of cholera spread through contaminated water and food, not through the 'miasma' of bad air. This understanding not only improved the management of an illness that periodically killed thousands, but stimulated public health and sanitation initiatives of benefit to all classes. Although aspirin was not known until 1897, developments such as anaesthetic (1847) and antiseptics (1865) made childbirth and surgical interventions more survivable. Yet these comforting signs of progress also precipitated spiritual crises. Because pain was no longer an inevitable part of human experience, it was more difficult to justify suffering as part of God's mysterious will, or to equate the physical torments of hell with the action of a loving creator. As in so many Victorian cultural forms, medicine became a site where science struggled with religion for authority over knowledge and truth.

Theories about the body–mind relationship were central to the growth of the 'mental sciences', an attempt to describe psychological processes in terms of physiological phenomena. Victorians knew from dreams and hallucinations that there were parts of the mind beyond the reach of consciousness. However, the Freudian model of the psyche and the modern science of psychology were unknown until the early twentieth century. Instead, the first practitioners of Victorian physiological psychology studied the physical mechanisms of mental activity in order to deal with individual aberrations. By focusing on the nerve processes that affected brain function, the mental sciences explained (away) behaviours deemed abnormal and showed how they might be disciplined and controlled. For instance, disruptive female attitudes and conduct were not linked to the frustrations and emotional damage of cultural oppression – though female writers knew better, as Charlotte Brontë suggested through her heroine in *Villette* (1853). Rather, such symptoms were diagnosed medically as hysteria or neurasthenia, pathological states arising from gynaecological and nervous ailments. The science of sexology, which developed in the last decades of the period, similarly invoked scientific method to identify and classify sexual preferences and behaviour, and thus establish norms. This framework served as a basis for 'diagnosing' alternative sexual identities – like homosexuality – as deviant 'inversions' of natural law that could be prevented or 'treated' to bring the individual subject into line with orthodox expectations.

The scientific approach to mental phenomena inflected Victorian literature. Fantasy and occult writing gradually focused more on psychological disturbance than on supernatural occurrences, as in George Eliot's clairvoyant novella, *The Lifted Veil* (1859), and Joseph Sheridan Le Fanu's (1814–73) hallucinatory short story, 'Green Tea' (1872). Spurious scientific fields like phrenology (the study of the skull to predict personality and intellect) and mesmerism also appealed to the literary imagination. Together with the more reputable sciences of the mind, they seemed to provide tools for penetrating social masks and controlling the deepest reaches of the personality, a theme explored in George du Maurier's (1834–96) novel *Trilby* (1894).

Human and social sciences

The human and social sciences helped to shape attitudes to cultural, racial and national differences. Archaeological research abandoned old-fashioned antiquarian methods, with their haphazard collection of artefacts from the past. It acquired an elaborate scientific apparatus, with emphasis on careful amassing of evidence, objective observation and analysis and the formulation and testing of hypotheses. Like many excavations in the period, Austen Layard's electrifying fieldwork at Nineveh (1845) extended an understanding of Western culture by uncovering a pre-classical past. Archaeological work at British sites, including Stonehenge, affirmed the steady progress of the nation by showing how native technologies evolved from flint to bronze and iron.

Philology, the comparative and historical study of language, together with the scholarly study of myths and religious systems, highlighted connections between cultures apparently separated by race and time. Alongside travel writing, archaeology and comparative religion, it contributed to the new interdisciplinary sciences of anthropology and ethnography. These fields helped Victorians to interpret the different cultures encountered through exploration and colonization. The influential anthropologist, Edward Tylor, pioneered the application of scientific techniques, including statistical analysis and classification, to the comparison of civilized and 'savage' customs and other social phenomena (Stocking 1996: 4). From this were deduced laws of cultural development, including the theory that many contemporary social, religious, and artistic practices had evolved from primitive rituals and beliefs.

Such approaches could narrow as much as enlarge public perceptions. Sociological studies, for example, made use of physiological, anthropological and ethnographic evidence (like facial expression, body shape and head size) to suggest the 'barbaric' nature of criminals, the mentally ill and other races. Using 'scientific' findings in this way both reinforced a sense of British cultural superiority and fuelled panic about the 'regressive' effects of violating cultural boundaries, by intermarriage, for example. Assumptions about other races (as superstitious, childlike, criminal and sexually rapacious, for instance) were elided with many kinds of cultural difference, such as 'other' classes (especially the working class) and 'other' nations (like the Irish or the Italians). Such stereotypes can be located in many popular literary forms of the period, including adventure yarns for children, such as R. M. Ballantyne's (1825–94) *The Coral Island* (1858), and for adults, including H. Rider Haggard's novels of African exploration, featuring Allan Quatermain.

Exploration

Investigation in order to understand, control and improve is one way of describing the goal of Victorian science. This principle also applied to the passion for exploration. Expeditions to mysterious parts of the globe, such as Africa and the Middle East, significantly extended botanical, zoological, geographical and anthropological knowledge. This in turn facilitated naming, mapping and systematically classifying other civilizations: it enabled mastery through knowledge. Victorians who journeyed into Africa – David Livingstone, a missionary; Henry Stanley, the journalist commissioned to find him; and John Hanning Speke, the explorer who sought the source of the Nile – demonstrate the spirit of earnestness, courageous adventure and scientific curiosity that characterized many Victorian expeditions. However, commercial exploitation of new territories was an unsavoury by-product. The profitable scramble for conquest and plunder was frequently carried out in the name of science, discovery and evangelization.

Exploration also made a darker impression on the Victorian imagination. From time to time, risky endeavours brought home the frailty of cultural boundaries. The disappearance of the Franklin Expedition to the Arctic in 1845 stimulated a number of rescue missions, numerous articles and a collaborative drama by Charles Dickens and Wilkie Collins, *The Frozen Deep* (1857). Even when it was clear that the expedition had been lost, the explorers' fate continued to exercise the public mind. Rumours suggested that some men had survived through 'the last resource' – that is, through cannibalism. The act itself was bad enough, but the failure of discipline that must have enabled such desperate measures raised particularly awkward questions about weak officers incapable of leading their men effectively. It appeared that, even in the sturdy heart of a Victorian Briton, savage instincts could overturn traditional patterns of authority and obedience.

Technology

Behind the most striking alterations in the Victorian physical milieu, working practices and leisure activities lay the technological application of science. Technology shaped the environment, contributing noise and pollution but also providing better transport systems, including the first double-decker omnibus (horse-drawn), a national railway network and the London underground. Manufacturing technology generated a vast proliferation of goods, and gave rise to new marketing venues like the department store. Inventions on both sides of the Atlantic, like the sewing machine and the Kodak camera, changed domestic life for many. Photography, for example, turned individuals into local and social historians, recording family, friends, daily activities and scenes, or, as in the portraits of Julia Cameron, into artists giving visual solidity to figures from legend and myth. While industrial technology played its part in creating the 'dark continent' of the slum, it also revolutionized work in large ways and small. Today we think mainly of immense factories and mechanized production; but even the invention of the typewriter altered administrative processes and opened up new careers for women.

Technology radically altered the experience of space and time. The telegraph, voice recording and the telephone – all Victorian inventions – gave an uncanny presence to the invisible and absent. Grandfather had existence beyond the grave when his voice could be heard emanating from the cylinder attached to the family gramophone, and ephemeral events – like a speech by Florence Nightingale or a reading by

Tennyson – were preserved for future generations, so that their influence quite literally 'lived on'. The telegraph overcame time and distance, to the benefit of businesses and the private individual. With the laying of a permanent cable link to North America in 1866, communications technology proved even vast distances could be 'conquered' by science.

Transportation technology similarly revised the Victorian sense of spatial connections. In 1845, for example, the first iron-hulled steam ship, *Great Britain*, made her maiden voyage to New York. Built by the greatest Victorian engineer, Isambard Kingdom Brunel, the *Great Britain* showed that transatlantic travel could be fast and safe, even in a vessel twice as big as any other ship ever seen on the seas. Such technological applications were central to maintaining British global superiority because they made access to distant lands reliable and quick.

Perhaps *the* most significant technological revolution of the period was the development of the British rail system. George Stephenson had invented his 'Rocket' steam locomotive in 1829, but Victorian entrepreneurial energies exploited its potential. In 1829 there were 51 miles of rail tracks in the country. By 1890, almost 13,000 miles connected most major centres and intervening towns and villages (Newsome 1998: 30). Trains moved thousands of passengers quickly about the country – though not always safely, as seen in Dickens's *Dombey and Son* (1846–8). Additionally, the railway boosted manufacturing by making it easier and quicker to move raw materials and finished goods in bulk, especially when visionaries such as Brunel, the creator of the Great Western Railway, integrated bridges and ships with the network.

The railway system certainly altered perceptions of time and space. The need for accurate timetables prompted Parliament to regularize all local times with Greenwich Mean Time. Isolated rural communities were drawn into the national mainstream through prompt rail delivery of post, newspapers and perishable goods. Massive track extensions restructured geography. Miles of cuttings sliced through countryside, and rail viaducts bisected city districts (stimulating urban redevelopment as a by-product). Quick transport enabled workers to live away from their place of employment in cheaper, outlying areas. The Victorian phenomenon of the suburb could not have occurred without the great expansion of the railway.

At first, Victorians feared that the speed of the train would draw the air from passengers' lungs and kill them. Tennyson – myopic and quite untechnical – fretted about the possibility of the carriage wheels leaping from the 'grooves' in the track. Ruskin despised the excursion trains bringing 'roughs' to his home in Herne Hill, where they knocked the fences about, disturbed the cows and pulled at the flower blossoms (1908: 48). But detractors and enthusiasts alike had to concede that, through the railways, Victorian Britain was transformed into the modern state we recognize today.

Not all Victorians embraced the scientific and technological revolution with equanimity. John Henry Newman, for example, remained sceptical that 'education, periodical literature, railroad travelling, ventilation, drainage, and the arts of life . . . [could] serve to make a population moral and happy' ([1864] 1968: 224). He had in mind the great spiritual challenges occasioned by science and the creeping secularism that seemed to accompany technological advance and prosperity. Undoubtedly, the wealth generated by technology did occasion – in some – greed, rapaciousness and indifference to others' suffering, while the new reverence for scientific method and evidence did – for others – strip away religious beliefs. A higher standard of living made for a measure of political complacency: more citizens were content with their lives and willing to support the status quo. Nonetheless, the benefits to the health and ease of life for ordinary people justified the knowledge revolution for many Victorians. As the essayist and critic Frederic Harrison (1831–1923) claimed about his century: 'It is *not* the age of money-bags and cant, soot, hubbub, and ugliness. It is the age of great expectation and unwearied striving after better things' (1886: 425). Science and technology first created, and then lived up to, that 'great expectation'.

2

Literature in the Victorian Period

MAJOR GENRES

Poetry

Introduction
Victorian poetry expressed the diversity of interests *and* uncertainties permeating contemporary culture: the struggle between faith and doubt; the emotional cost of love and rejection; the contrasts between country and city; the desire for freedom and the nobility of duty and self-sacrifice. Stylistically, Victorian poetry demonstrated changing artistic values. Early in the period, high moral seriousness was inseparable from traditional ideas of poetic beauty realized in rich imagery, evocative language, mellifluous sound and established forms. Gradually, technical elegance was supplanted, sometimes by a more prosaic register, sometimes by eccentric

innovations and sensuous experimentation that suggested style was important for its own sake, crafted for the pleasure of reader and poet regardless of subject.

Despite its variety, Victorian poetry was consistently viewed as an art form with profound significance. As the poet and critic Matthew Arnold argued, poets guided culture by offering contact with 'the great primary human affections' (1972: 29). Through its seriousness, beauty and truth, poetry addressed 'the question, *how to live*' ([1888] 1911: 142). Victorian poets acknowledged this responsibility in different ways. The Poet Laureate, Alfred Lord Tennyson, spoke directly to his age as an inspiring prophet and preacher, com-mitted to middle-class ideals. Arnold, a liberal humanist, pre-sented calm analysis, reflecting the peculiar isolation and self-consciousness of his intellectual milieu. Even in the last decades of the period, when many poets professed them-selves indifferent to public interests and moral purpose, poetry continued to enlarge the reader's understanding. Capturing those ephemeral impressions that constituted consciousness, *fin-de-siècle* lyrics dramatized the very sensa-tion of living. This work had value as 'the voice of a human soul' (Symons [1893] 1968: 904).

Voice is a potent metaphor, indicating the importance, for Victorians, of subjective experience and the individual's feelings and sensations. As a result of their Romantic inheritance, early Victorians saw poetry as a mode of self-expression, giving privileged access to 'feeling, confessing itself to itself in moments of solitude' (Mill 1981: 348). As self-revelation, it also conveyed what was unconscious, sup-pressed or veiled, communicating 'some hidden emotion' or 'yearning desire' (Keble 1912: 5–6). In time, the poetic representation of feelings like alienation, ennui and despair evolved into criticism of contemporary life. Moreover, in expressing the unmasked inner self, Victorian poetry articu-lated viewpoints normally excluded from other social discourses. By writing new voices into the cultural script, Victorian poetry held the strange and the familiar in a stim-ulating tension.

The lyric

The dominant Victorian poetic genre was the lyric, focused most usually on themes of nature, love, religion and death. In terms of tone, lyric poetry was occasionally ecstatic, frequently stoic, but most often self-consciously sad, regretful and, sometimes, despairing. Favouring bleak or bitter-sweet introspection, Victorian lyricism was primarily elegiac, expressing nostalgia for lost happiness and meditating on flux as the essential quality of the modern human condition. Alfred Tennyson and Matthew Arnold are the most celebrated poets in this vein. In 'Tears, Idle Tears', from Tennyson's *The Princess* (1847), blank verse and an accretion of similes represent regret for the irretrievable past as haunting and pervasive, but inexplicable. Matthew Arnold's 'Stanzas from the Grande Chartreuse' (1855) analyses the reasons for such melancholy. Caught between a 'dead' Christian culture and an unknown future world, 'powerless to be born', the speaker envisages himself wandering aimlessly in an uncertain, transitional state. Even 'Two in the Campagna' (1855), by the more optimistic Robert Browning, expresses typical Victorian longing, since the meeting of lovers presages inevitable parting and the sorrow '[o]f finite hearts that yearn'.

Early and mid-Victorian lyric melancholia stressed the spiritual ramifications of loss and despair. In Tennyson's elegy, *In Memoriam* (1850), sorrow for a dead friend leads to meditation on the meaning of death and the afterlife. The poem's 130 lyrics compare the stages of personal bereavement (from pain to hope) to the intellectual passage from doubt about God's existence to belief in His Providence. 'Thyrsis' (1867), Arnold's pastoral elegy commemorating the poet Arthur Hugh Clough, also connects mortality and the 'mute' artist to the loss of faith. While the idealistic poet will always seek truth, the 'harsh, heart-wearying roar' of modern life provokes sadness and resignation. Similarly, in 'The Scholar Gipsy' (1853), Arnold diagnoses spiritual emptiness as the disease of his society, 'with its sick hurry, its divided aims'.

The despairing tone typical of Victorian lyricism gradually refocused on the psychological ramifications of lost confidence, whatever its cause. Stylistic innovations accompanied the growing interest in emotional trauma. In George Meredith's sonnet sequence about a disintegrating marriage, *Modern Love* (1862), an experimental 16-line sonnet form, linguistic compression and a dense web of allusions suggest the psychosexual turmoil of the betrayed husband persona. In the so-called 'Sonnets of Desolation' (1885/7) by Gerard Manley Hopkins, depression is expressed through abrupt, violent language and metaphoric precipices of the mind, '[f]rightful, sheer, no-man-fathomed' ('No Worst'). At the end of the period, Thomas Hardy's ironic lyric voice suggests disillusionment as the modern psychological norm. Through indirection and understatement, 'The Darkling Thrush' (1900) conveys the barren scepticism with which late Victorians faced the new century.

Indeed, such stylistic virtuosity and variety is characteristic of the Victorian lyric. Second-generation Romantic poets, such as John Keats (1795–1821), had set the standard for poetic beauty in the first half of the nineteenth century. Early Victorian lyrics demonstrate 'Keatsian' attributes: seductive, lush poetic diction, complex metres, inventive rhyme schemes and figures of speech, picturesque imagery and a taste for classic poetic forms, like the pastoral and the ode. Tennyson's 'The Lotos Eaters' (1842) is typical; while the mythological subject is 'Victorian' in its stress on work and duty, the luxuriant style highlights 'Romantic' pleasure in sensuous indulgence. Similarly, his luscious descriptions in 'Now sleeps the crimson petal' (1850) add a sexual subtext to a decorous, romantic invitation to love.

Victorian lyricists routinely borrowed the beautiful natural settings, idealized past and exotic lands of Romantic poetry, but used them differently. Sometimes, these features heighten the mood of elegiac nostalgia. In Browning's 'Home-Thoughts from Abroad' (1845), an English spring generates pathos because its beauties, previously neglected, are now out of reach. The delightful pastoral setting of Arnold's

'The Scholar Gipsy' (1853) points up the rough struggle, heartache and 'mental strife' of modern experience. His 'Dover Beach' (1867) alludes to classical Greece in a reflection on the 'long, withdrawing roar' of the Victorian 'Sea of Faith'. This envisaging of the present through the lens of the past, seen also in Arnold's meditation on the myth of the nightingale in 'Philomela' (1853), brings consolation by suggesting heroic predecessors experienced similar anguish over lost ideals. On the other hand, the lyrics of Dante Gabriel Rossetti (1828–82) and William Morris, the Pre-Raphaelites, employ meticulously detailed settings that heighten the 'authenticity' and 'reality' of the experiences portrayed, but also 'encode' the inexpressible. In Rossetti's 'Silent Noon', from the love sonnet sequence *The House of Life* (1870), languorous descriptions of a lush field on a hot summer's day are analogous to the sensations of erotic passion. The unfamiliar landscape of Morris's 'Iceland First Seen' (1891) defines heroic values long vanished from England.

As these last examples might suggest, luxuriant poetic detail had an increasingly controversial function in the last half of the period, undercutting bourgeois moral and artistic values, particularly when addressing the question, 'how to live'. For example, sensuous descriptions and a fatalistic tone in *The Rubáiyát of Omar Khayyám* (1859), Edward Fitzgerald's (1809–83) free rendition of an ancient Persian text, commend indulgence as the melancholic solution to life's brevity. By the late 1880s, a more impersonal lyric voice often detached images from clear 'meaning' altogether. In Oscar Wilde's 'Symphony in Yellow' (1889), for example, fog and the polluted Thames are incorporated into a beautiful impressionist pattern that has no significance other than its own spare elegance. By 1900, 'how to live' was no longer about principles and behaviour, but about cultivating a sensitive delight in beautiful form, however fleeting or contrived it might be.

Experimentation in diction and verbal effects also transformed the lyric, most notably in the move from the melodic and elaborate to the prosaic and spare. The traditional metres, rhyme patterns, language and verse forms characteristic of some early Tennysonian works, such as the song of 'The Sea-Fairies' (1830), were replaced by a dispassionate, stoic voice, more flexible syntactical structures and undecorated language that mimicked spontaneous thought, as in Arnold's 'Self-Dependence' (1852) and 'Rugby Chapel' (1867). Pastiche and parody were always part of the Victorian poetic scene, as exemplified by Clough's cynical 'The Latest Decalogue' (1849). But the later taste for a cool, contemplative style added depth to this mode. In 'Shelley's Skylark' (1887) by Thomas Hardy, a pared-down vocabulary is central to ambivalent mockery of Romantic visionary effusiveness. The same understated technique made late Victorian lyric pessimism, such as that of A. E. Housman's sequence, *A Shropshire Lad* (1896), seem particularly poignant.

In the last half of the century, stylistic experimentation also reflected the Victorian fascination with intense emotional states. Technical virtuosity goes hand-in-hand with religious fervour in the work of two Catholic poets, Francis Thompson (1859–1907) and Gerard Manley Hopkins. Thompson's bizarre images, Latinate words (some invented) and tortured syntax highlight spiritual anguish and ecstasy, as in 'The Hound of Heaven' (1893), where the fast-paced sequence of baroque conceits depicts the soul's abjection in the face of God's relentless pursuit. Although virtually unpublished in his lifetime, Hopkins profoundly influenced twentieth-century poetics, especially through his linguistic inventiveness and Sprung Rhythm, a metrical form based on stresses (rather than syllables) in each line. His monumental ode on a maritime disaster, 'The Wreck of the Deutschland' (1876), is a brilliant compendium of unconventional poetic strategies. Startling rhymes, new compound words, odd line breaks, surprising images, exclamations, compressions and omissions project the paradox of a terrifyingly majestic and delicately loving Deity: 'Our hearts' charity's hearth's fire, our thoughts' chivalry's throng's Lord'. His 1877 nature lyrics, including 'The Windhover',

'Pied Beauty' and 'Spring', are similarly innovative, albeit more accessible.

On the other hand, an intense emotional experience *for the reader* lies at the heart of Algernon Swinburne's dazzling, exhibitionist style. Luscious rhymes and mesmerizing rhythms entrance the ear and seductively promote radical sexual, religious and political views in the lyric choruses of *Atalanta in Calydon* (1865), as well as in works from *Poems and Ballads* (1866) and *Songs before Sunrise* (1871). Swinburne's 1866 collection stirred particular controversy due to its irreligious pessimism ('The Garden of Proserpine'), but also because it so melodiously inverted good and evil, sexual pain and pleasure, love and death ('Satia Te Sanguine', that is, 'Satiate thyself with blood'). In their beautification of the morbid, perverse and blasphemous, and in their relish for illicit desires, Swinburne's lyrics prefigure the poetry of the Decadent movement, including work by Ernest Dowson (1867–1900) and Lionel Johnson (1867–1902).

Victorian lyrics exercised significant cultural influence, particularly in the construction of gender identities, and especially femininity. For example, Coventry Patmore's popular sequence, *The Angel in the House* (1854–61), idealized *and* subjugated woman as the emotional and spiritual core of the family. By representing her as a silent 'paragon' to be adored but also as a 'foreign land' never to be understood, the male speaker effectively wields power as the interpreter of the female subject. Even Dante Gabriel Rossetti's sonnet sequence, *The House of Life*, thought shocking in its 'sacred' worship of erotic passion, nonetheless reproduced conventional images of womanhood: beloved inspiration or sinister *femme fatale*.

However, women lyricists offered a different account of the emotional experience of their sex. Working in familiar female territory – religion, love and death were common themes – they revealed the pathos of women's subordinate position from the 'inside'. L.E.L. (Letitia Landon) (1802–38) concentrated on the grief of the tragic, deserted woman; Augusta Webster (1837–94) subtly conveyed the dullness and depression of a woman's lot ('In the Pamfili-Doria Gardens', 1893); and Alice Meynell (1847–1922) hinted at passionate longing beneath dignified self-denial ('Renouncement', 1875, and 'After a Parting', 1890). Whether radical or conservative, Victorian women poets made use of the lyric's capacity for subtle, poignant expressiveness to protest against the limitations imposed upon them. The socialist feminist poet, Amy Levy, projected a melancholy, modern consciousness out of joint with the world (*A London Plane-Tree and Other Verse*, 1889). Lesbian love was celebrated by Katherine Harris Bradley (1846–1913) and Edith Emma Cooper (1862–1914), who wrote collaboratively as 'Michael Field'. Even the poetically conventional Adelaide Proctor (1825–64), famous for her sentimental poem-hymn 'A Lost Chord' (1860) (set to music by Arthur Sullivan), suggested that female emotional horizons were more complex than traditionally acknowledged.

The most accomplished female poets of the period, Elizabeth Barrett Browning and Christina Rossetti, might seem conventional enough in their focus on self-sacrificial commitment to human and Divine lovers. However, their lyrics re-evaluated the nobility of female selflessness and suffering. Rossetti's 'The Triad' (1856) and 'Eve' (1865) dramatize the psychological damage done by women's internalization of imposed gender models; and numerous love poems and religious lyrics draw ambiguously on feminized patterns of obedience and sacrifice ('Remember Me', 1862; 'Weary in Well-doing', 1864). Barrett Browning's work challenges acceptable 'norms' more overtly. 'The Cry of the Children' (1843) argues against child labour in mines and factories, while her two sonnets dedicated 'To George Sand' (1844) praise the cross-dressing female novelist's transgression of gender boundaries that traditionally kept women silenced and invisible.

Like Sand, both Barrett Browning and Rossetti unite male originality – 'a poet-fire' – with a passionate 'woman-heart', qualities evident in their innovative handling of traditional poetic forms. In Barrett Browning's *Sonnets from the Portuguese*

(1850) and Rossetti's 'Monna Innominata' (1881), the gender
values normally embedded in a love-sonnet sequence are
questioned by replacing the traditional male voice with a
female one. Off her pedestal, the usually silent beloved can
express a woman's insecurities and ecstasies in courtship. While the speakers of both works ultimately remain
self-sacrificing women, Barrett Browning's eroticism and
Rossetti's handling of love as betrayal and retreat bring
female desire to the fore.

Dramatic verse

Dramatic verse appealed to the Victorians' fascination with
the human personality, and the dramatic monologue – a
form in which a character is revealed in conversation with an
implied, silent listener – appealed most of all. Robert
Browning was pre-eminent in this genre, producing works of
subtle psychological insight. His rough diction and rhythmic
inventiveness in both rhymed and blank verse create collo-
quial voices that seem authentic and unique. Browning's
most famous monologues – in *Dramatic Lyrics* (1842), *Dramatic
Romances and Lyrics* (1845), *Men and Women* (1855) and *Dramatis
Personae* (1864) – ironically expose the speakers' strategies of
self-protection and self-deception in hiding or disguising
particular feelings. Because Browning's characters unconsciously betray their own failings, the reader is forced to
evaluate, not just empathize with, the personality behind
the voice.

Such critical judgement is facilitated by Browning's frequent use of 'distanced' speakers from past and foreign cultures. Yet the traits they disclose shed light on Victorian
attitudes, too. In 'My Last Duchess' (1842), the sixteenth-
century Duke veils a possessive, misogynistic and cruel
nature with the kind of refined taste and manners that many
middle-class Victorians mistook for moral worth. Ruskin, for
one, admired Browning's capacity to sum up the corruption
of the Renaissance in 'The Bishop Orders His Tomb at Saint
Praxed's Church' (1845), but these ramblings of a dying
Catholic prelate also reveal the hypocrisy of religious cant

and the dangers of materialistic greed – phenomena apparent in Victorian society. Browning also excelled in the portrayal of character types from his contemporary world. Particular beliefs, as well as personalities, are criticized through the smug hypocrisy of the tricky 'Mr Sludge, "The Medium" ' (1864) and the cynical Catholic leader in 'Bishop Blougram's Apology' (1855). Neither character is convinced of the 'creed' he imposes on his followers.

On occasion, the Victorian dramatic monologue offered 'protection', distancing unconventional views from the poet while making them seem comprehensible, even admirable. In 'Pictor Ignotus' (1845), 'Fra Lippo Lippi' (1855) and 'Andrea del Sarto' (1855), Browning in effect defends his own dense, unmelodious style, suggesting that artistic brilliance depends on rejecting dead conventions. The pathos of 'The Runaway Slave at Pilgrim's Point' (1848) enables Elizabeth Barrett Browning to argue for the abolition of slavery in America, while the voice of a Roman pagan gives Swinburne 'cover' for an attack on Christianity in 'Hymn to Proserpine' (1866). With this capacity to draw the reader into an unusual perspective, the dramatic monologue also appealed to Victorian poets wishing to elicit understanding for the marginalized. A number of monologues, for example, express sympathy for prostitutes and fallen women, such as Dante Gabriel Rossetti's 'Jenny' (1870), Augusta Webster's 'A Castaway' (1870) and Amy Levy's 'Magdalen' (1884). Women's inequality in society is the central grievance of each speaker in Webster's 'Circe' (1870) and Levy's 'Xantippe' (1880). Although Rudyard Kipling's *Barrack-Room Ballads* (1892) invoke the discourse of late-Victorian imperial patriotism and downplay the violence of colonization, they too work against the grain by giving voice to the forgotten (but essential) working-class soldier who defends the Empire ('Tommy') and by expressing admiration for the 'first-class fightin' man', whatever his race ('Fuzzy-Wuzzy').

The ironic gap in dramatic monologues between the reader's understanding and the character's stated views makes it an apt form for exploring abnormal psychological states. In the most interesting Victorian examples, the dividing line between normal and extreme perspectives seems very fine, with the disquieting implication that orthodoxy and irrationality have something in common. For example, the mad speakers of Browning's 'Porphyria's Lover' (1836) and 'Soliloquy of the Spanish Cloister' (1842) hold some conventional views on women and sensuality. Tennyson's stylistic experimentation in 'Locksley Hall' (1842) suggests that the speaker is as much disturbed by the pressures of a materialistic society as by unrequited love. In the lengthy, morbid 'monodrama', *Maud* (1855), Tennyson blends lyric, dramatic and narrative elements to depict the psychological deterioration of the embittered speaker, tormented by the commercialization of modern culture.

Narrative poetry and the long poem

Victorian narrative poetry drew on folktales, ballads, and literary material as well as contemporary events to portray moments of high passion or psychological distress, as in Tennyson's atmospheric 'Mariana' (1830) and 'The Lady of Shalott' (1842) or Dante Gabriel Rossetti's art ballad, 'Sister Helen' (1853). Sentimentality was one way of heightening the emotional effect. Adelaide Proctor's 'Philip and Mildred' (1861) concludes with a heart-wrenching death-bed scene as comment on the Victorian practice of long betrothals. Presenting heroism in action also provided emotional satisfactions for readers seeking nobility in the face of violence, baseness and flux. Arnold's 'Sohrab and Rustum' (1853) advocates stoicism through the poignant tale of a father who inadvertently destroys his son. Familiar characters, or character types, from fairy-tales, legends and mediaeval romances, offered Victorian readers an opportunity to evaluate different moral positions in narrative poems exploring life's temptations. William Morris's 'The Defence of Guenevere' (1858) and Christina Rossetti's 'Goblin Market' (1862) make use of the strategy, pitting ideals of self-denial, love and honour against the real workings of sexual desire, though the poems reach different conclusions.

It was the Victorian long poem – usually narrative in mode – that most fully responded to the demand for literature that would explain 'how to live'. Borrowing the novel's interest in the social environment and character development over time, the form dealt expansively with private and public life. While Clough's *The Bothie of Tober-na-Vuolich* (1848), about Oxford students on vacation, gently satirized contemporary social attitudes, his *Amours de Voyage* (1858) offered an in-depth examination of failed commitment in love and politics, pointedly using the Italian struggle for state unity as a thematic backdrop. Other outstanding long poems engaged with topical debates: the higher education of women (Tennyson's *The Princess*); the woman poet as commentator on modern life (Barrett Browning's *Aurora Leigh*, 1857); the disillusionment with 'civilized' values and 'the spreading of the hideous town' (Morris's *The Earthly Paradise*, 1868–70). Poets welcomed the form's flexibility for developing complex ideas. Robert Browning's *The Ring and the Book* (1868–9), for example, reconstructs a sensational seventeenth-century Italian murder through multiple dramatic monologues. The poem suggests uncomfortable parallels between the snobbery, greed and cynicism of late Renaissance Rome and the bourgeois attitudes of Victorian Britain. However, by juxtaposing different interpretations of the central action, Browning also challenges Victorian confidence in 'facts'. That the same story *must* be told from different angles in order to establish the morality of the case shows that surface details should never be mistaken for truth itself.

Some long poems explored modern culture through allegory, indirection and analogy. Clough's poetic drama, *Dipsychus* (1865), imaginatively displaces the divided, alienated Victorian mind onto a series of debates between an idealist and the Spirit of worldly values. Morris's violent Norse saga, *Sigurd the Volsung* (1876), reveals the poet's socialist sympathies in its revolutionary overthrow of greedy rulers and its hero's support for the lowly. Perhaps the most famous of all Victorian long poems is Tennyson's *Idylls of the King* (1859–85), a monumental 12-book epic based on Arthurian legend. The poem invites a multi-dimensional reading that accommodates contemporary social parallels (Arthur is at one point compared to Prince Albert), the promotion of idealized models of gender, citizenship and nationhood, and a more philosophical debate about the aspirations of the Soul and the needs of the Flesh.

Poetry by and about the working classes

Not all Victorian poetry engaged with middle- and upper-class voices. Anonymous street ballads and protest songs expressed the perspectives of working people in their mockery of topical subjects including 'The Cotton Lords of Preston', the Great Exhibition and the 'saturation' celebrity of Prince Albert. There was no 'peasant poet' to match the Romantic John Clare (1793–1864); but the Dorset farmer's son (and, ultimately, Cambridge graduate) William Barnes (1801–86) produced fine dialect poetry, or country 'lippings' in Hardy's phrase (Cunningham 2000: 79). To portray the godless urban milieu, James Thomson eschewed realism in favour of surrealistic effects in *The City of Dreadful Night* (1874). In this nightmare kingdom of 'Melencolia', Gothic landscapes, hallucinatory images and a slow, monotonous style particularly suit the inhabitants, who have become apathetic ghosts or primeval monsters.

Middle-class poets also addressed the plight of the downtrodden. The crusading journalist Thomas Hood (1799–1845), favoured melodrama and sentimentality. The remorseless 'stitching' beat of 'The Song of the Shirt' (1843) and the quick-paced rhymes and rhythms of 'The Bridge of Sighs' (1844) heighten the pathos of the pitiful sweat-worker and the suicidal fallen woman respectively. 'The March of the Workers' (1885), by William Morris, is an instance of direct political campaigning, predicting the overthrow of capitalism and the return of power and creativity to the 'people'. With their Biblical inflections and hymn-like diction, Morris's socialist poems have much in common with the earlier writing of working-class Chartist poets, including Thomas Cooper (1805–92).

Victorian poets also celebrated the 'invisible' worker. Hopkins's sinewy diction and metre evoke the rugged body of the farm labourer in 'Harry Ploughman' (1887) and the physical energy of the stout-hearted British navvy in 'Tom's Garland: Upon the Unemployed' (1887/8), evidencing, perhaps, a homosocial gaze. Lightness of touch defines the Decadent incorporation of the working class into an aestheticized realm. Arthur Symons's (1865–1945) drunken, mad, dancing 'Nora on the Pavement' (1894) is the product of social injustice and indifference; but her embodiment in a delicate poetic artefact suggests that she too possesses a beautiful integrity worthy of contemplation.

When Arnold predicted poetry would replace religion as an inspirational force, he could not have imagined today's fading interest in the form. On the face of it, the respect for courage, self-control and endurance typical of Victorian poetry at large seems alien to the downbeat relativism currently in fashion. Yet the diversity and innovation of Victorian poetry, its determined rejection of the commonplace in art and life, suggest it still has much of relevance to say about 'how to live'.

Fiction

Introduction

Fiction – particularly the novel – replaced poetry as *the* most influential and popular Victorian literary form. Part of its appeal was its relevance. Mainstream fiction dealt with the matter of everyday life. Even historical novels represented versions of society recognizable to the growing number of literate consumers. A familiar world, mediated in an uncomplicated prose style, was populated by engaging characters who grappled with the same problems of self-formation and moral choices that readers felt they faced too.

Fiction also dominated the literary scene because it was more readily available, through cheaper books (thanks to mechanized printing technology), borrowing rights (thanks to subscription libraries), and instalment purchase (thanks to

serialization in separately bound issues or in monthly magazines). The unexpectedly high sales of Charles Dickens's
serialized novel, *The Pickwick Papers* (1836–7), showed the
potential of part-publication, and many important Victorian
novelists, including Thackeray, Gaskell, Trollope and Hardy,
adopted it for at least some of their works. Moreover, serial
publication reached an even wider cross-section of the
Victorian public than sales figures suggest due to the growth
of reading circles where members listened to or shared instal-
ments. Because the novel united social groups in a unique
way, it came to be seen by writers, readers and critics as an
important instrument of cultural influence.

Serial publication shaped *how* writers wrote, as much as
what they wrote. A typical Dickens novel ran over 19 monthly
parts of 32 pages, with a double instalment in the final
number. Feedback to author and publisher was immediate,
via correspondence and purchasing statistics, and this shaped
the actual process of composition. Unpopular characters
could be quietly dropped, and well-received sub-plots fleshed
out. Particular strategies reflected novelists' new obligation to
hang on to their readers. Each issue had to provide excitement and development, but still leave mysteries and sus-
penseful situations for resolution in future numbers.
Characters, settings and plotlines had to be memorable to
allow for the time-gap between each issue. Reliance on
caricatured visual appearances (a favourite technique of
Dickens), catchphrases, recurrent image strands and the
cliffhanger climax were all prominent narrative devices that
met these needs.

The diversity of readers also influenced style and technique. Classical and foreign allusions that assumed substantial formal education were downplayed in favour of
contemporary references. The forms and themes of popular
culture, including melodrama and fairy-tale, ensured readers'
connection with the material. To suit family audiences, violence and sexuality were discreetly rendered. Readers were
not patronized, however. Dramatized scenes, rather than
authorial summary, became the norm, forcing readers to

exercise evaluative judgement. Victorians approached novel-reading as a process of decoding. They expected fiction to delight, but also to inform, challenge and sharpen their interpretation of a complex cultural environment.

Realism and Victorian fiction

By far the most typical mode of Victorian fiction is that of realism, an ideologically complex form incorporating many bourgeois assumptions about the world. From the commercial enterprises of Dickens's *Dombey and Son* (1846–8) to the rural communities of George Eliot's *Adam Bede* (1859) and Thomas Hardy's *Far from the Madding Crowd* (1874), from the hostile labour relations in Charlotte Brontë's *Shirley* (1849) and Gaskell's *Mary Barton, a Tale of Manchester Life* (1848), to the church politics in Anthony Trollope's *Barchester Towers* (1857), realist fiction seemed to offer a transparent window onto a society in rapid transition. Of course, while all these writers could be said to work in the realist tradition, their novels are different in style, approach and theme. Realism is neither uniform nor static, but changes as views about 'reality' itself change. Victorian writers and reviewers shared some assumptions about the realist novel: its commitment to presenting the 'truth' of 'real' life; its dialogue with other types of prose fiction; and its dual concern with the social milieu and the reality of the individual consciousness. But the handling of these features altered over the period.

Early Victorian novels enhanced the novel's 'truth to life' through formal features. For example, Charlotte Brontë presented *Jane Eyre* (1847) as an 'autobiography', edited by an authoritative 'male' figure (her pseudonym, Currer Bell). Her sister, Emily Brontë (1818–48), used 'eye-witness' recollections to suggest the authenticity of events in *Wuthering Heights* (1847). The hybrid nature of realism is evident here, too. Recognizable landscapes are juxtaposed with the extreme plots and character types of earlier romance fiction, highlighting the difference between the surface 'reality' of genteel manners and the 'elemental' truth of intense passion. From mid-century, the fiction of Dickens, Gaskell, Eliot and

Trollope constructed reality more broadly. Through such devices as multiple viewpoints, omniscient narrators who comment and guide, and complex plots with a number of intertwining personal 'histories', novels such as *Bleak House* (1852–3) and *Middlemarch: A Study of Provincial Life* (1871–2) provided a panoramic perspective. Changes in social structures, beliefs and expectations were explored through characters who exploited – or were victimized by – powerful institutions and vested interests.

From the 1860s, psychological realism began to dominate the form. George Eliot was particularly influential in suggesting that 'reality' was a subjective construction, created, at least in part, by the individual's personal interpretation of events. In addition to *Middlemarch*, Eliot's pastoral novel *Silas Marner* (1861), historical novel *Romola* (1863) and final novel, *Daniel Deronda* (1876), show the moral subtleties achieved by relocating action to the 'inside'. From this point, the novel more commonly balanced the external 'reality' of social situations with the interior 'reality' of conscious impressions and unconscious impulses, as in the introspective tragedies of Henry James (1843–1916), including *The Portrait of a Lady* (1881). Thomas Hardy (*The Woodlanders*, 1887) and George Gissing (*New Grub Street*, 1891) explored subjectivity from a different angle, showing how a brutal social environment constrained and crushed the inner 'reality' – the dreams and aspirations – of the protagonists. Indeed, this central Victorian preoccupation – the tension between an individual and society – informed other sub-divisions of realism, most notably the Bildungsroman and the 'Condition of England' novel.

The Bildungsroman

A German form – the Bildungsroman – is often viewed as *the* model of realist fiction. Although no equivalent English word exists for this novel of personal maturation from childhood, the genre had particular affinity with the Victorian investment in self-formation, which explains its popularity. The Bildungsroman demonstrates middle-class confidence in the individual who can learn from experience and, through initiative and effort, occupy a respectable place in society. Loyalty, self-control and personal responsibility are important values emphasized in Victorian versions of the genre.

What every realist novel attempts to do for its reader, the plot of the Bildungsroman does for its protagonist: that is, replace a false (mistaken) view of the world with a true (mature) one. Typical Victorian examples, such as Dickens's *David Copperfield* (1849–50) and *Great Expectations* (1860–1) and Thackeray's *The History of Pendennis* (1848–50), differentiate clearly between childish misapprehension and a sound moral insight, normally coinciding with middle-class ideals about individual success and social duty. Although Bildungsroman narratives by women, including Brontë's *Jane Eyre*, Eliot's *The Mill on the Floss* (1860) and Amelia Edwards' *Barbara's History* (1863), also emphasize individualism, they depict female maturation as a process of self-realization rather than self-correction. Their heroines often point up the gap between a woman's 'true' sense of self and society's 'false' expectations of her; yet in the end, their destinies are conventional.

The 'Condition of England' or social problem novel

Most Victorian realist novels address a 'problem' of one kind or another. Even love stories explore 'real' dilemmas, such as Anne Brontë's *The Tenant of Wildfell Hall* (1848) with its marriage of a faithful woman to a dissolute husband. The 'social conscience' of Victorian fiction is seen in themes drawn from contemporary social failings: repressive educational systems in Dickens's *Nicholas Nickleby* (1838–9) and *Hard Times* (1854) and George Meredith's *The Ordeal of Richard Feverel* (1859); the treatment of fallen women in Gaskell's *Ruth* (1853) and Collins's *The New Magdalen* (1873); and the folly of monetary greed in Dickens's *Our Mutual Friend* (1864–5). However, the Victorian social problem novel, emerging from about 1840, places particular emphasis on the increasing gulf between rich and poor, employers and the working class.

In 1839, Carlyle coined the term, 'Condition of England Question', to highlight the human and social cost of industrialism and aggressive economic policies. The phrase is now used for Victorian novels on this theme, such as Dickens's *Oliver Twist* (1837–9) with its depiction of the operation of the New Poor Law and workhouse system, and of the urban conditions giving rise to delinquency and a criminal underclass. Like many social problem novels, including Gaskell's *North and South* (1854–5), Dickens's work sidesteps the case for a radical change to class structures, relying instead on the reconciling plots of marriage and reunited families. Often, the genre suggests that the worst effects of industrial capitalism can be ameliorated through middle-class values: moderation, good sense and a reliance on mutual understanding.

Some 'Condition of England' novels are undoubtedly more politically engaged. By dramatizing the gulf in England between the rich and the poor in *Sybil, Or The Two Nations* (1845), Benjamin Disraeli could present the advantages of aristocratic paternalism and 'One Nation' Toryism, compared to the dangers of radical Chartist action. Christian Socialism is promoted in Charles Kingsley's *Alton Locke, Tailor and Poet* (1850) through the unusual device of a cockney hero (who rejects violent Chartist revolution in favour of Christian love and service). Eliot's *Felix Holt, The Radical* (1866) illustrates the genre's gradual evolution into the novel of social ideas, concerned with the principles and philosophies that should underpin reform. Written at the time of the Second Reform Bill, the narrative assesses whether moral development of 'the people' or legislation is the more effective means of securing working-class progress.

The novel of public life

The Victorian novel of public life focuses on the operation of the great Victorian institutions: church, politics, law and business. Unlike the 'Condition of England' novel, this genre is less concerned with the opposition of the bourgeoisie and proletariat than with the subtle social gradations and interactions within the middle class in its broadest sense: the shopkeeper, the man of commerce, the educated professional and the country squire. George Eliot's *Middlemarch* draws on these relationships to suggest the limitations of Victorian society for the cultured intellectual. However, the novels of Anthony Trollope might be said to be more truly representative of the genre in their sympathy for the middle-class ideals of social stability and personal dignity, and in their criticism of the backbiting struggle for position within the professional world. His series of linked novels – the Barsetshire novels (1855–67) and the Palliser novels (1865–80) – explore ecclesiastical and political institutions respectively.

Historical fiction

The Victorian interest in the past as both nostalgic ideal and the seed of present mischief fed fiction. While most major novelists produced at least one historical novel, none achieved the eminence in the genre of Walter Scott (1771–1832), although Thackeray's *The History of Henry Esmond* (1852) is regarded as one of the outstanding historical novels in English. Based on meticulous research into eighteenth-century cultural life, Thackeray's narrative is an impressive representation of the social and political milieu under Queen Anne. Generally in this genre, however, the setting is a transparent excuse for promoting Victorian values or commenting on contemporary issues. Dickens's *Barnaby Rudge* (1841) (about the anti-Catholic Gordon Riots of 1780) and *A Tale of Two Cities* (1859) (about the French Revolution) evidence a topical interest in the 'manliness' of chivalric self-sacrifice, the rights and wrongs of capital punishment, and the possibility of 'mob' violence arising from exploitation of the masses. Charlotte Brontë's *Shirley* (based on the Yorkshire Luddite protests of 1811) and George Eliot's *Romola* (set in fifteenth-century Florence during the rise of Savonarola) have several obvious parallels to Victorian culture, with their portrayal of civil unrest and strong-minded, passionate women in conflict with society's expectations.

That said, novels that reconstructed the past as sensational – all crime, sex and violence – also gripped the Victorian imagination as a titillating contrast to the respectable present. Scenes of pagan debauchery and sadistic torture, together with plots of treachery and doomed romance, give melodrama precedence over historical accuracy in such novels as Edward Bulwer-Lytton's (1803–73) *The Last Days of Pompeii* (1834), Wilkie Collins's *Antonina* (1850), Kingsley's *Hypatia* (1853) and Charles Reade's *The Cloister and the Hearth* (1861).

Religious fiction

George Eliot may have called them 'hateful', but explicitly religious novels were a mainstay of Victorian literature (Maison 1961: 2). Serious novelists, little read today but well regarded in their time, found narrative impetus in the joys and pains of belief and doubt. Charlotte Yonge, for example, a novelist with Tractarian sympathies who wrote for adults and children, concentrated on the trials of family life in *Hopes and Fears, Or Scenes From the Life of a Spinster* (1860) and *The Clever Woman of the Family* (1865). Although the novels do not preach, they validate Christian teaching by combining romance plots with those of repentance, dutifulness and pious endurance. Christian self-sacrifice and charitable love are central to her best-selling *The Heir of Redclyffe* (1853), much admired by serious literary figures, including William Morris and Rossetti. Another prolific writer, Margaret Oliphant, explored religious problems in her 'Chronicles of Carlingford' series. The fourth novel, *The Perpetual Curate* (1863–4), demonstrates Oliphant's skill in deriving serious interest from denominational factionalism. Like Trollope's Barsetshire novels, the Carlingford sequence has its fair share of ecclesiastical rivalry and competition, but also raises trenchant points about belief and conversion. In 1888, Mary Ward responded to the general mood of spiritual uncertainty with *Robert Elsmere*, the sensitive portrayal of an earnest man who transforms religious doubt into social action. Drawing on Ward's unhappy family experience of Catholic conversion, *Helbeck of Bannisdale* (1898) explores another topical faith struggle: the trauma caused when a fervent, austere Catholic falls in love with a principled sceptic.

Religion haunts the periphery of many 'secular' Victorian novels. Catholicism is both a social 'fact' and a metaphor in Charlotte Brontë's *Villette* (1853), the sign of an alien patriarchal culture in which the heroine must assert her 'heretic narrative' of female independence and equality ([1853] 1979: 235). Dickens (and even the Unitarian Elizabeth Gaskell) are typical of the great realists who 'generalized' the Christian spirit in a way that would appeal to readers of any and all denominational leanings (and none). They ignored doctrine in favour of humane values that would create ethical social relations – kindness, endurance and decency. From time to time George Eliot alluded to the compassion, courage and dutifulness of exemplary Christians, including St Teresa and Thomas à Kempis, but she maintained an agnostic distancing from their supernatural beliefs. At the end of the period, Thomas Hardy angered some readers with his overt criticism of religious bigotry and hypocrisy in *Jude the Obscure* (1895), though he contended that many shared his attitudes.

Comic fiction and satire

Victorian satiric and comic fiction is essentially a hybrid genre, portraying real follies, but drawing stylistically on the picaresque, parody and burlesque for breadth of canvas, humorous diversions, and ready-made caricatures that add to the fun and mockery. Dickens's *The Pickwick Papers* offers a panoramic frolic through an affectionately idealized Merry England; yet even the jolly escapades of Samuel Pickwick and his fast-thinking cockney sidekick, Sam Weller, have their blacker moments (in Fleet Prison, for example). Thackeray's serial, *The Snobs of England* (1846–7), resembles *Pickwick* in its format: an episodic journey through English society following the adventures of Mr Snob (the 'snobographer'). However, the sharp dissection of English pretentiousness and mean-mindedness in Thackeray's work (which endowed 'snob' with the meaning we give it today) bites more aggressively than Dickens's essentially optimistic narrative. *Vanity Fair* (1847–8) built on Thackeray's *Snobs* success, employing a modified picaresque structure to attack the leisured middle class with its rising expectations fuelled by avarice, duplicity and hypocrisy. The contrasting female characters – the aptly named Becky Sharp who cuts moral corners to succeed and the dutiful, long-suffering Amelia Sedley – follow different trajectories, but Becky's survival suggests her kind of corruption can no longer be eradicated.

Later Victorian writers, equally offended by smug inhumanity and hypocrisy, employed a variety of narrative forms to demolish staid assumptions through bitter laughter. Trollope's broad-brushstroke, multi-plot satire, *The Way We Live Now* (1874–5), is uncharacteristically cynical in its attack on 'dishonesty' in literary and financial circles, in love and politics. Samuel Butler's (1835–1902) *Erewhon, or, Over the Range* (1872) eschews realism for a dystopian inversion of middle-class priorities in a country that is both an anagram of 'nowhere' and an acid parody of Victorian Britain. Butler's *The Way of All Flesh* (1903), masquerading as a popular family 'saga' of the generations, exposes Victorian domestic ideology as a tyrannical farce. George Meredith targeted the archetypes of the gentleman and the respectable woman, exposing their two-faced sentimentality through a generous application of 'the comic spirit', by which he meant the cool revelation of false ideals. Stylistic density, melodramatic plots, witty sarcastic aphorisms, and unconventional frankness in dealing with sexual experience and gender relations made Meredith's 'comed[ies] of narrative', like *The Egoist* (1879) and *Diana of the Crossways* (1885), disagreeable reading for some contemporaries.

Naturalism

Naturalism also resisted comfortable middle-class assumptions. To a casual reader today, the novels of the French Naturalist, Émile Zola (1840–1902), might seem almost indistinguishable from realist fiction in their concern with physical detail, careful charting of social experience and unflinching commitment to authenticity. However, the Naturalist movement opposed the Victorian certainties encoded in realist conventions, such as the capacity of individuals to change and improve their lot, and the essentially harmonious and beneficial nature of society.

George Moore was the first prominent British novelist to declare his Naturalist tendencies, although the work of George Gissing and Thomas Hardy has some Naturalist elements. Moore's *A Mummer's Wife* (1885), tracing the squalid career of an actress, was notorious. Its topics of adultery, divorce and alcoholism prompted Mudie to ban the writer's work from his circulating libraries. *Esther Waters* (1894), the gruelling tale of a working-class girl seduced in service, was equally frank (and quite successful). Hardy adapted Naturalist and Darwinian principles to the late-Victorian novel. While *Under the Greenwood Tree* (1872) and *A Pair of Blue Eyes* (1873) have a regional charm, Hardy's major works are stripped of pastoral serenity, notwithstanding his sympathetic depiction of country folk. *Far from the Madding Crowd* (1874) initiates a sombre narrative series set in a fictionalized south-west England called 'Wessex'. Relentlessly plotting the destruction of individuals' hopes, the Wessex novels characterize contemporary life as the hopeless struggle for survival against the impersonal powers of nature and society, so that pessimism seems the only rational response to the 'ache of modernism' ([1891] 1988: 129). In *The Return of the Native* (1878), *The Mayor of Casterbridge* (1886), *Tess of the D'Urbervilles* (1891) and *Jude the Obscure* (1895), allusions to a hostile 'fate', plots of coincidence and sensational disasters (including rape, adultery, child murder and suicide) suggest that success and self-improvement are matters of chance and always short-lived. For a middle-class readership seeking endorsement of cherished ideals, this was altogether too strong stuff. After the hostile reception of *Jude the Obscure*, Hardy abandoned the writing of fiction for poetry.

Popular fiction

Middle-class readers did not always prudishly eschew 'something hot and the strong' (Mansel 1863: 485). That is the description one reviewer applied to the phenomenally successful 'sensation fiction' that flourished from the late 1850s to the 1870s. Actually, many best-selling Victorian works adopted the 'sensation' formula of shocks, suspense and titillation, neatly circumscribed by the final restoration of moral order and respectability. While today we tend to make a distinction between 'literary' fiction and popular 'genre' fiction, nineteenth-century writers and readers did not draw such sharp boundaries. Queen Victoria enjoyed the novels of Scott, Disraeli, Trollope and Eliot, but also snapped up the bizarre occult romances of Marie Corelli (1855–1924) like *Ardath, The Story of a Dead Self* (1889). Major literary figures, including Dickens and Margaret Oliphant, wrote in such popular forms as ghost stories and, throughout the period, many novelists with social, political and psychological points to make – from Charlotte and Emily Brontë to Arthur Machen (1836–1947) and Robert Louis Stevenson (1850–94) – made use of Gothic fantasy in their omens and occult dreams, their creepy settings, their incarcerated mad wives and haunting doubles.

Eighteenth-century Gothic fiction, with its supernatural elements and diabolical plots of victimized heroines, parental tyrants and thwarted heirs, may have provided some symbols in mainstream novels, including Dickens's *Great Expectations*, but it mainly resurfaced in popular culture of the day. G. W. M. Reynolds (1814–79) wrote for lower-class readers who craved excitement dressed up as contemporary investigative journalism. His serialized *Mysteries of London* and *The Mysteries of the Court of London* (1845–55) owed more to lurid Gothic and melodramatic romances than to any objective reporting. These weekly exposés of the dissolute horrors of the 'Modern Babylon', including grave-robbing 'resurrection men', dissipated aristocrats and assorted lawbreakers, were laced with the additional *frisson* of anti-establishment republicanism. Lower down the fictional scale were the 'penny dreadfuls' and 'penny bloods' that rehashed clichéd plots of crime, violence and horror. This cheap pulp fiction was aimed particularly at the pocketbooks of the credulous, newly literate poor.

For more sophisticated readers, Gothic images, plots and character types recirculated in sensation fiction, horror novels and supernatural tales, but characteristically, these genres off-set fantastic elements with realist attention to the material details of everyday life and to plotting based on pseudo-scientific explanations, such as mesmerism in George du Maurier's *Trilby* (1894). Because such strategies anchored these novels firmly in their historical moment, they reveal much about Victorian cultural contradictions. 'Sensation fiction', for example, capitalized on curiosity *and* anxiety about the depravity concealed within the respectable Victorian home and institution. Certainly, the sensationalism embedded in Collins's *The Woman in White* (1859–60), *Armadale* (1864–6) and *No Name* (1862–3) and Mary Elizabeth Braddon's *Lady Audley's Secret* (1862) and *Aurora Floyd* (1863) made these compulsively readable narratives; and, despite their racy subjects, they elicited the strong approval of readers (though not critics). Mrs Henry Wood's *East Lynne* (1861) was so successful it was adapted as a stage play, and a number of writers tried out sensation fiction as a way of giving their early careers a boost, as 'Ouida' did with *Strathmore* (1865) and Hardy with *Desperate Remedies* (1871).

To Victorians, sensation novels seemed an artfully crafted version of those scandalous narratives that sustained the popular press: illegitimacy, fraud, false identity, the imprisonment of the sane in mental asylums, bigamy, murder. However, today's scholars are fascinated by the way they ambivalently undermine *and* reinforce mid-Victorian views about the stability of identity and social boundaries. Fast-paced and tricky in plotting, adventurous in the use of multiple narrative voices and unreliable protagonists, with passion and secrecy as powerful motivators and mystery and suspense as plot-engines, these works – especially those of Collins – enact cultural uncertainty by thwarting traditional narrative conventions and playing against the reader's expectations.

While sensation fiction offered (often improbable) rational explanations for surprising occurrences, Victorian fantasy explicitly celebrated the marvellous and the uncanny. Established writers could see the popularity of the genre in the public's enthusiasm for the Grimm brothers' fairy-tales (translated in the 1820s), eighteenth- and nineteenth-century adaptations of *The Arabian Nights* and the stories of Hans Christian Andersen (1805–75) (translated in 1846) – hence, Ruskin's *The King of the Golden River* (1851), Thackeray's *The Rose and the Ring* (1855) and Wilde's *The Happy Prince and Other Tales* (1882). Charles Kingsley's *The Water-Babies* (1863), George MacDonald's (1824–1905) *Phantastes* (1858) (for adults) and *At the Back of the North Wind* (1868–9) and *The Princess and the Goblin* (1870–1) (for children), as well as Lewis Carroll's (1832–98) *Alice's Adventures in Wonderland* (1865), demonstrate the rich experimentation in the field, including adroit handling of surreal effects, escapist nonsense, and psychological and social allegory. Social issues (like sanitation reform) are incorporated seamlessly into Kingsley's moral-religious tale; the spiritual and psychological dimensions of growing up are central to MacDonald's work; and the juxtaposition of the playful and philosophical ensures Carroll's adventure novel can be read on many levels.

Ghost stories appealed to the same Victorian pleasure in the fantastic, but science and social awareness gave the genre a more pointed cultural application. Dickens's *A Christmas Carol* (1843), for example, passes over the religious implications of tormented spirits to comment on the evils of selfish acquisitiveness, and the importance of empathy and generosity, while his short story, 'The Signalman' (1866), associates doom with modern technology (the railway). The growing interest in the significance of occult and psychological phenomena also nuanced the development of the genre. Early Victorians were content to establish the 'reality' of such occurrences, as in Catherine Crowe's (1800–76?) *The Night Side of Nature* (1848), a record of supernatural 'happenings', hauntings and apparitions. But, in the last half of the century, ghost stories offered a vehicle for speculating about the unconscious. Dread, horror, suspense and the occult in Joseph Sheridan Le Fanu's *The House by the Churchyard* (1863), *Uncle Silas* (1864) and the female vampire story, 'Carmilla' (1872), actually focus attention on characters' psychological states, mental aberrations and obsessions. *The Strange Case of Dr Jekyll and Mr Hyde* (1886) by Robert Louis Stevenson and *The Turn of the Screw* (1898) by Henry James are perhaps the best-known examples of psychological ghost fiction, using familiar generic conventions to consider the power of mental distur-bance and unconscious impulse. While Stevenson employs a stock character – the *doppelgänger* – to suggest the psychotic multiple personality, James focuses on a single consciousness as it 'sees' or 'imagines' the external world. James's impres-sionistic, elusive style suggests that frustration, insecurity and uncertainty are the demons of the modern mind.

The Victorian tradition of the spooky ghost story as Christmas entertainment showed a nation collectively prepared to delight in a fright, though authors used the form for more than 'pure' entertainment. For some ghost-story writers – among them, Charlotte Riddell (1832–1906), Margaret Oliphant and Amelia Edwards – 'weird' powers spoke of forces beneath everyday life that could easily 'possess' the unwary and over-anxious. In the last decades of the nineteenth century, the ghost story mutated into the more extreme tale of horror, highlighting cultural degeneration, perverse sexuality, and even, as in Stoker's *Dracula* (1897), fears about miscegenation. In *A Phantom Lover* (1886) and *Hauntings* (1890) by Vernon Lee (1856–1935) and *The Great God Pan* (1894) by Arthur Machen, the occult is combined with a Decadent outlook. These fictions of erotic terror iden-tify social decline and psychological fragmentation as the 'spirits' haunting the *fin de siècle*.

Other forms of popular fiction display similar cultural specificity, though their plots of suspense and discovery make them highly readable as well. For example, the conventions of the new genre, detective fiction, express the Victorian yearning for stability and authority in a complex world requiring careful decoding. Thus, Inspector Bucket in Dickens's *Bleak House* (1852–3) draws on the rising profile of the Victorian policeman as investigator. Wilkie Collins's *The Moonstone* (1868) is often considered the first detective novel in English, because it first used the now familiar pattern of clues and red herrings, scientific analysis and brilliant, logical deduction to solve a crime. Readers skilled in following the ingenious plots of sensation fiction and attuned culturally to the 'magical' power of modern science especially appreciated the genre, which explains the extraordinary popularity of Arthur Conan Doyle's (1859–1930) Sherlock Holmes stories that began in 1887.

Discovery through adventure connected fictional entertainment to serious social comment. The scientific romances of H. G. Wells – the first forays into science fiction – challenged many Victorian attitudes through their distinctive combination of the marvellous, the 'factual' and speculations about the future. An exciting encounter with new worlds is central to *The Time Machine* (1895), *The Island of Dr Moreau* (1896) and *The War of the Worlds* (1898). However, Wells's imaginative blend of evolutionary theory, scientific jargon, realist narrative methods and utopian themes ensures stories of danger and survival also make readers reflect on contentious issues: the cruelty of vivisection, the oppression of the proletariat and the dubious morality of imperialism.

Swash, buckle, thrust and parry enlivened the novel of imperial adventure, which, unlike science fiction, presented a more upbeat view of the glories of Empire. This genre made much of the dangers encountered by the daring men who tamed the wilderness for profit, glory and the Mother Country, epitomized by H. Rider Haggard's big-game hero, Allan Quatermain, in *King Solomon's Mines* (1885). Unlike the historical romances of Robert Louis Stevenson, such as *Treasure Island* (1883), *Kidnapped* (1886) and *The Master of Ballantrae* (1889), with their quests and rivalries, treachery and feuds, Haggard's novels encode the worst elements of colonial racism. *She* (1886–7), for example, represents native peoples as hostile and savage, given to unspeakable bestial practices and sorcery. Joseph Conrad's bleak depiction of white exploitation in the Congo in *Heart of Darkness* (1902) offered a response to such ideologically charged narratives.

Rudyard Kipling's tales of India also tapped into Victorian imperial experience, keeping the interests of the Mother Country to the fore. His *Jungle Book* volumes (1894/5), animal fables for youthful readers, romanticize the native child of nature, Mowgli, and promote racial tolerance, though implying the colonizer's essential superiority. The Anglo-Indian short stories, such as those in *Plain Tales from the Hills* (1888), explore English problems (such as domestic infidelities) rather than Indian society per se, despite their exotic locations. The picaresque novel, *Kim* (1901), uses the 'street Arab' stereotype for Kipling's Irish boy-hero who passes easily between Anglo and Indian culture; once 'civilized', he serves British interests through the 'game' of espionage. By the early twentieth-century the imperial adventure was supplanted by the novel of international intrigue (Anthony Hope's (1863–1933) *The Prisoner of Zenda*, 1894, being a precursor). This generic development mirrored new political alliances and a shift in the balance of international power against Britain.

Despite the craze for sensation, mystery and adventure, Victorian popular fiction was not solely obsessed with the extreme and the exotic. When Trollope praised novels offering 'a picture of common life enlivened by humour and sweetened by pathos' ([1883] 1974: 109), he described the domestic romance. Without sinister foreigners and murderous deeds, the genre delighted readers with its meticulous attention to the familiar rhythms of everyday existence: adolescence, courtship, love and parting. Serious Victorian writers had always understood the importance of these subjects, as Gaskell's unfinished *Wives and Daughters* (1864–6) attests. At the popular end, however, domestic fiction endorsed, rather than probed, mainstream values, endorsing ideals of masculinity and femininity, the innocence of childhood and the importance of the family unit. Even the best practitioners of middle-brow domestic fiction, like Charlotte Yonge (*The Daisy Chain*, 1856) or the racier Rhoda Broughton (1840–1920) (*Not Wisely But Too Well*, 1865–6), affirmed the primacy of duty, family solidarity and social discretion.

In its concern with manners and etiquette, Victorian domestic fiction actually owes something to the earlier 'silver-fork' school of fiction that flourished between the 1820s and 1840s and is best exemplified by Disraeli's *Vivian Grey* (1826–7), Bulwer-Lytton's *Pelham* (1828) and Catherine Gore's (1799–1861) *Cecil* (1841). Concerned primarily with the sensibility and conduct of the aristocratic and fashionable 'set', 'silver-forkery' entertained by revealing the secrets of the modish. Inevitably, as middle-class tastes and mores dominated society, the genre became a source of parody. However, its elitist mannerisms wittily resurfaced in the late-Victorian cult of the dandy, seen in Wilde's *The Picture of Dorian Gray* (1890/1).

Henry James once termed Victorian novels 'large, loose, baggy monsters' (1935: 84). He had in mind their predilection for vast, complex plots, a host of characters, and the panoramic display of social gradations and intersecting communities. Certainly, the breadth and diversity which James spots, evident in style, theme and genre, is a response to changing social conditions, to the transformation of communities, beliefs and behaviour in an expanding industrial nation. Whether adhering to mainstream conventions or ingeniously constructing fresh narrative methods, Victorian fiction represents a culture under pressure, both desiring and fearing a new social order.

Drama

Introduction

Today we know Victorian drama from the witty, socially aware early plays of George Bernard Shaw (1856–1950), the sparkling comedies of manners by Oscar Wilde, and the good-humoured patter of Gilbert and Sullivan. However, this is a fraction of the Victorian dramatic repertoire. Victorian theatre also revelled in a spectacular materiality, specializing in excess and display made possible by advanced technology. Sumptuous lighting, costumes and stage properties, together with elaborate crowd scenes, ingenious plotting and sentiment by the bucketful characterized much popular dramatic output of the period. Thanks to stagey larger-than-life extravaganzas and pantomimes, showy and educational historical pageants and moving romantic melodramas, the Victorian theatre held its own in the highly competitive entertainment 'industry' that developed in cosmopolitan centres. Threatened by rival attractions, including dioramas, Continental imports like Italian ballets and operas and even scientific displays, Victorian theatre rose magnificently to the challenge. But evolution is also part of Victorian theatre history. Balancing the taste for the ever more lurid and luxurious, domestic drama and the problem play gradually asserted the importance of subtlety, realism and contemporary social themes.

The theatre of spectacle

Early Victorian drama reflected the peculiarities of the licensing laws that regulated theatres. Before 1843, only two theatres in London were permitted to stage straight plays, including Shakespeare, while other venues had to mix dramatic elements with at least five musical interludes. Often based on mutilated versions of famous plays, including those by Shakespeare, these *burlettas* set a trend for light, fantastic and amusing drama based on familiar stories and characters. They are closely allied to the fairy-tale extravaganzas, comic burlesques and glamorous pantomimes, such as those by James Robinson Planché (1796–1880) and H. J. Byron (1834–84), which drew large audiences throughout the period. These forms in turn became excessively elaborate, incorporating dancing troupes, minstrel shows and comic turns rivalling music-hall variety programmes. But the work of craftsmen like Planché, who retained his popularity from the 1820s to the 1870s, had influence as well as mass appeal. His combination of spectacle with more or less logical plots and a topical mood was developed in more sophisticated form by Gilbert and Sullivan's witty Savoy Operas, including *The Pirates of Penzance* (1879) and *Iolanthe* (1882).

The abolition of the patent monopoly system in 1843 transformed audiences, theatres and drama itself. Squalid pits with backless benches and beer sellers were refurbished as the expensive stalls area with padded seats and carpeting. Rowdy 'pittites' were removed to the galleries, and suddenly, even the elegant middle class found theatre-going an enjoyable, fashionable activity. In 1851, 20 theatres could be found in London. By 1900, there were 61 London theatres, all demanding fresh sensations and new material (Booth 1980: 31). As entertainments became more diverse, different kinds of venues catered for different class tastes. Music halls attracted the widest range of working- and lower-middle-class customers, but the audiences for straight plays also expanded to include not only the aristocracy and fashionable 'set', but also all ranks of the mobile middle class.

Given the wider audience-base, theatre managers sought accessible material with broad appeal. Best-selling novels, like Harriet Beecher Stowe's *Uncle Tom's Cabin* (1851–2), were adapted for the stage, as well as works by Walter Scott, Bulwer-Lytton, Wilkie Collins and Charles Dickens. From the 1840s, theatre writing drew on genres that had familiar plots (such as farce) or that appealed to emotion rather than intellectual debate (such as melodrama). For example, Dion Boucicault (1822–90) appropriated the racy and cynical language, plots and character stereotypes of Restoration Comedy to great effect in his comedy, *London Assurance* (1841). His more complex romantic melodramas mixed the natural and theatrical in dealing with history (*The Corsican Brothers*, 1852) and his Irish inheritance (*The Colleen Bawn*, 1860, and *The Shaughraun*, 1874). In addition to sensationalized elements, hackneyed situations and picturesque settings, they included individualized oddities of character and scope for realistic special effects.

Stage conditions also influenced the development of Victorian drama. The original barn-like patent theatres invited a mannered, static and declamatory style of delivery with coarsened gestures, ranting speech and broadly drawn characters. But when straight drama could be offered in more intimate spaces, acting – and plays – could employ greater emotional subtlety. New lighting techniques made optical illusions especially powerful. The move from wax candles to limelight (an intense white light achieved by burning lime in a special flame), then to gauze around gas jets, and finally, to the incandescent bulbs of the late-Victorian theatre increased the possibilities for greater realism (and improved safety). With the darkened theatre the norm by 1850, clever lighting could simulate storms, ship-wrecks, ghosts and fiery conflagrations. By the end of the century, ever more imaginative application of engineering science, including hydraulics, meant bravura aquatic specta-cles, train crashes, horse races and even earthquakes could be replicated, although, as one drama critic complained about a lively production in 1888, '[i]t would require lungs of leather to shout louder than the din of carpenters and scene-shifters' (Booth 1965: 173).

Advances in costume design and scenic painting encour-aged more informative kinds of 'authenticity'. The vogue for 'archaeological' productions, like the *Henry VIII* (1855) and *Richard II* (1857) of actor-manager Charles Kean, made the most of gorgeous pageantry, large crowd scenes, and meticu-lous detail in costumes and accessories to assert historical accuracy. By displaying the results of scholarly research (often bolstered by elaborate programme notes and reading lists), these works promised education as well as entertain-ment. Yet such picturesque lavishness shifted attention away from plot and characterization; it seemed unimportant that Shakespearean texts were cut and rearranged to accommo-date complicated scene changes. With new value attached to the *mise en scène* (or overall performance design), the Victorian director, rather than the leading actor, gradually became the powerful interpretative force driving the production.

Melodrama and sensation

Early melodramas that played largely to working-class and lower-middle-class audiences, like those of the prolific Edward Fitzball (1793–1873), employed spectacle for startling and heart-wrenching effects. Touching death scenes or last-minute escapes moved the sympathies of the audience. The moral schema was uncomplicated and dialogue and action were unsubtle: 'She's mine! She's mine, mine! – Editha! Cold, cold, dead!' (Reynolds 1936: 130). We might treat Victorian melodrama as an object of curiosity, but this dramatic form, popular throughout the Victoria era, influenced weightier genres, especially in its conflation of the serious, the sensational and the sentimental.

Victorians were less embarrassed by emotional excess than we are today. Tears of joy and 'sweet sorrow' at another's situation were taken as a sign of moral sensitivity and benevolence (Houghton 1957: 276). Many character-based melodramas, such as W. B. Bernard's (1807–75) *The Passing Cloud* (1850), thus cultivated pathos from obvious themes such as the conflict between love and duty, a topic later given greater psychological depth in more substantial domestic dramas. For example, in *Saints and Sinners* (1884) and *The Case of Rebellious Susan* (1894), Henry Arthur Jones (1851–1929), one of the most respected Victorian playwrights, generated dramatic tension from the individual's struggle to accommodate personal desire to social respectability.

As well as enjoying tear-jerking moments, early Victorian audiences relished melodramatic shocks, especially when these were based on topical scandals and crimes. The runaway hit of the 1830s, *Maria Marten; or, the Murder in the Red Barn*, was based on a notorious homicide case, for instance. The 'factual' reality added to the nerve-jangling excitement, but it also encouraged audiences to appreciate plays referring explicitly to the social environment, even within the far-fetched conventions of melodrama. Reforming themes were thus incorporated into the popular theatre. Douglas Jerrold's (1803–57) *The Rent Day* (1832) satirized the rich who exploited the poor and the starving. Although wooden and lacking in subtlety, such plays anticipated the more realistic approach to social issues in mid-Victorian drama. The most popular melodrama of the century, Tom Taylor's (1817–80) *The Ticket-of-Leave Man* (1863), centred on contemporary low-life and drew extensively on familiar social settings (a busy public tea-garden) and character types (Hawkshaw, the private detective). Despite caricature and the reliance on such creaky devices as disguise and coincidence, the concern with social conditions and injustice in popular drama shaped the tastes of Victorian audiences, preparing the ground for the social problem plays of Arthur Wing Pinero (1855–1934) and George Bernard Shaw.

Victorian melodramas intended for more sophisticated audiences, such as Boucicault's *Formosa; or, the Railroad to Ruin* (1869) and Jones's *The Silver King* (1882), used the sensational to interrogate social and psychological problems. They frequently revealed respectability as, quite literally, a 'performance', easily faked. Villainy shocked because it was disguised by masculine charm and feminine delicacy. These dramas hitched the familiar devices of sensation fiction, such as mistaken identity, to vividly realized scenes of fashionable life – the Oxford-Cambridge Boat Race, for instance – or to contemporary bourgeois nightmares, including train crashes and police pursuit of the innocent. Their themes suggest a Victorian middle-class preoccupation: the impossibility of knowing, and hence trusting, others on the basis of appearances alone. Sensational elements probed the realms of the unconscious as well as external manners. The haunting pain of a guilty conscience, for example, was central to Leopold Lewis's (1828–90) *The Bells* (1871) and represented by impressive scenic effects, supernatural manifestations, and the mesmerizing, eccentric acting style of Henry Irving. This instant success showed how public taste was shifting: the 'real' drama of the inner self handled symbolically was now as thrilling as spectacular events.

Domestic Realism and social problem plays

The counterbalance to spectacle and sensation was a new realism of an understated, domestic kind. Squire and Marie Bancroft, the husband–wife actor–manager team that took over the Prince of Wales's theatre in 1865, popularized 'credible' playwriting with their staging of 'cup-and-saucer' dramas. Taking their name from the incorporation, on stage, of humdrum activities such as making tea or mixing up pudding batter, these works evidenced subtleties of theme and characterization that more overt staginess missed. Tom Robertson's (1829–71) *Society* (1865), *Ours* (1866) and *Caste* (1867) exemplify the genre. Each play developed character and addressed social problems through a clear, simple plot, natural – sometimes even trivial – dialogue, and fidelity to everyday customs. Robertson made use of the three-walled box scene, or 'picture stage' (rather than wings and scenic backdrop), to replicate the rooms of modest middle-class homes; and the starkness of his titles hinted appropriately that directness, rather than flamboyance, would characterize the tone. This is not to say that these works lack emotion or neglect ethical issues. But their poignancy is derived from the ordinary: human beings struggling to negotiate personal happiness amid such obstacles as class boundaries. Robertson broke new ground by abandoning sentimental formulae, but his plays conservatively endorsed the existing social system and Victorian Evangelical morality.

George Bernard Shaw's late-Victorian plays were indebted to the anti-romantic style of low-key realists like Robertson, especially in characterization and plot structure, but Shaw transformed domestic drama through acid wit and a socialist conscience. His radical approach to social issues illustrates the revolutionary impact of the Norwegian playwright, Henrik Ibsen, on the Victorian literary scene. The unforgiving depiction of establishment hypocrisy and self-righteousness in Ibsen's *Pillars of Society*, first performed in Britain in 1880, shocked theatre-goers more accustomed to the reaffirmation of cherished ideals. However, Ibsen's exposure of the falseness of middle-class ideology appealed to Shaw's political perspectives, and he set about composing plays that would entertain and discomfort at the same time. *Widowers' Houses* (1892), for example, not only revealed the exploitative nature of capitalism that preyed on the poor, but also suggested no one was immune from its corrupting influence. *Arms and the Man* (1894) debunked the romance of war; and *The Devil's Disciple* (1897) used an anti-romantic hero to attack the hypocritical Church. Most provocative of all was *Mrs Warren's Profession*. Written in 1894, the play was banned as obscene until 1924 because it depicted a prostitute as a capable businesswoman, implying that all wealthy people in a capitalist system lived off the proceeds of immoral practice.

Other late-Victorian dramatists also courted controversy by following Ibsen and venturing to deal seriously with the 'unpleasant'. Arthur Wing Pinero, the first man knighted solely for playwriting, established his reputation as a farceur and crafter of sentimental comedies with *The Magistrate* (1885). However, in a series of tragedies and problem-plays he confronted contentious social issues. *The Profligate* (1889) investigated the sexual double standard for men and women, while *The Second Mrs Tanqueray* (1893) challenged the nature of sexual prejudice, focusing on the exclusion of a woman with a past from respectable society. It is important to note that, despite her reformation, Mrs Tanqueray is not accepted. Pinero maintained his popularity by disturbing, but not wholly disrupting, the beliefs of his audience. Henry Arthur Jones, on the other hand, managed to disturb *and* disrupt in his late, highly naturalistic dramas addressed to the Victorian intelligentsia. His realistic dialogue and expertly handled dramatic tension did not soften his social critique. *Saints and Sinners* (1884) offended many with its attack on Puritanical morality as hypocritical; and *Michael and His Lost Angel* (1896), about an adulterous *and* censorious clergyman, was forced to close after a ten-day run.

Comedy of manners

It was with the elegant late Victorian comedy of manners that social criticism, craftsmanship and wit came most successfully together, neither causing rejection and outcry, nor leaving the audience's pretensions unpricked. In the course of the period, the early nineteenth-century French concept of the *pièce-bien-faite* (the well-made-play) had been adapted for British upper-class audiences. A small cast of bourgeois characters, a few loyal servants, an obstacle or two, an unexpected and clever resolution, fashionable idioms and contemporary settings and costumes were essential to the formulaic treatment of love and marriage. Oscar Wilde exploited these features in *Lady Windermere's Fan* (1892), *A Woman of No Importance* (1893), *An Ideal Husband* (1895) and *The Importance of Being Earnest* (1895). Peppered with sparkling epigrams, these works employ frivolity, modishness and a rapier-like wit to expose the moral compromises and intellectual clichés of the self-regarding, fashionable Victorian establishment. The less sophisticated light operas of Gilbert and Sullivan tread a similar path, using good humour, nonsense and absurd situations to mock everything from military incompetence (*The Pirates of Penzance*) and civil service bureaucracy (*The Mikado*, 1885) to the artifice and mannerisms of effete aesthetes like Wilde himself (*Patience*, 1881).

Victorian critics and reviewers were aware that a theatrical revolution had taken place during their lifetime, and that drama had become a major literary institution, shaping public taste and the public conscience. In Matthew Arnold's word, theatre had an 'irresistible' appeal, but also a social importance because it satisfied the need 'for expansion of spirit, for intellect and knowledge, for beauty, for social life and manners' (1973: 80). By the end of the period, the director and the playwright had new stature and power; artistic and social values were as central as profit to many writers, theatre managers and audiences; calls for the removal of censorship and the clarification of copyright law to protect authors were increasingly vociferous. Within this framework of change, revival and reform, Victorian theatre finally occupied the place cinema would hold in the twentieth century. Intellectually dignified *and* popular, it offered entertainment and cultural challenge to an audience hungry for its delights.

Non-fictional prose

Introduction
Avidly consumed by the intelligentsia *and* the general reader, non-fictional prose helped to fashion the Victorian self-image and underpinned imaginative writing through its ideas, themes and images. Ranging from the upbeat and optimistic

to the critical and despairing, this work captures the diversity of nineteenth-century views about society and its problems, and illustrates how, in every field of 'factual' knowledge, beliefs and values were explicitly in competition. Moreover, while responding to the Victorian drive for knowledge and improvement, non-fictional prose served as cultural criticism. Whether focused on public life and the progress of the nation (in 'sage writing', for example) or drawing on private experience (in life writing and travel narratives), it shared the restless quest to understand the contemporary 'condition' that permeated all Victorian literary forms.

History, sage writing and public commentary

In the nineteenth century, engagement in public life meant writing about it. W. R. Greg (1809–81), a civil servant, reviewer and essayist, was typical. Beginning as a radical supporter of the Reform Act and finishing his career as an opponent of such liberal causes as women's entry into the professions, Greg contributed extensively to the literature of public comment and social analysis, offering his opinions on diverse social, economic and political matters, including 'redundant women' (spinsters) and prostitution. The attention paid to his diagnoses of social ills (in *Rocks Ahead, or, The Warnings of Cassandra*, 1874, for example) shows the lingering Victorian respect for the authoritative 'generalist' in public life and for the tradition of *belles-lettres* (fine writing on literary and intellectual topics). Such prose contributed significantly to Victorian cultural self-consciousness.

History writing commented upon contemporary culture more indirectly. Many of the most revered historical works promoted a view of British nationality and the British 'character' that endorsed Victorian values: progress, individualism and material prosperity. Thomas Babington Macaulay's *History of England* (1849/55) assessed the past and present optimistically. The compelling prose style, telling characterization and strong narrative line that recorded the 'great and eventful drama' of the nation appealed to a readership pleased with itself, its enlightened reforms and its wealth creation ([1849] 1906: 11). Numerous historians followed Macaulay's lead. James Anthony Froude's *History of England from the Fall of Wolsey to the Defeat of the Spanish Armada* (1870) confirmed the superiority of the nineteenth-century (Protestant) establishment, by suggesting the Protestant Reformation accounted for the nation's success and strength. John Richard Green's (1837–83) popular *Short History of the English People* (1874) fixed on the doughty English temperament as the reason for the country's continuous progress. It was mainly late Victorians, such as Edward Carpenter (1844–1929) in *Civilisation: Its Cause and Cure* (1889), who took issue with such interpretations. Maintaining his reputation as a supporter of radical causes, including anti-vivisection and women's rights, Carpenter used history to debunk, rather than celebrate, the Victorian investment in entrepreneurship, reason and will power. For him, material progress represented the triumph of selfishness over the harmonious, intuitive connection with the living spirit of nature.

The greatest Victorian prose writers – Mill, Carlyle, Arnold, Ruskin and Newman – have been dubbed 'sage' writers: social prophets, critics and moralists. Their specialist disciplines (politics, philosophy, literature, art, theology) were vehicles for elucidating values appropriate to a crisis-ridden society. For example, John Stuart Mill's *Principles of Political Economy* (1848) set out the ideals of radical liberalism based on private property and *laissez-faire* economics, but also argued that social and political reform was required for a just, stable community. In *On Liberty* (1859) and *The Subjection of Women* (1869), he extended these principles to encompass civil rights for those traditionally marginalized or constrained by narrow-minded, middle-class attitudes. Indeed, all Victorian sage writers challenged the strong 'compliance culture' of their day, especially its encouragement of greed and self-interest. Although they proposed different solutions, they shared a desire for social renewal that was ethical and, in some sense, spiritual. Carlyle's Idealist 'Life-Philosophy', Arnold's humanism, Ruskin's proto-socialism, and Newman's Catholicism were offered as alternatives to the excessive value placed on materialism, prosperity and advancement.

As one of the earliest Victorian 'sages', Carlyle was most indebted to Romanticism, particularly German Transcendentalism. In 'The Signs of the Times' (1829), 'Characteristics' (1831) and *Sartor Resartus* (1833–4), he denounced the mechanistic philosophies of rationalism and empiricism, arguing instead for a concept of work that united individuals and aligned them with the spiritual energy animating the cosmos. His explosive style with its eccentric metaphors, aggressive outbursts, invented words and illogical connections expressed a fear of violent upheaval arising from social injustice. *Chartism* (1839), for instance, predicted proletarian revolution because the propertied classes had failed to shoulder their civic responsibilities. Increasingly contemptuous of democratic liberalism that seemed to encourage idleness and a shirking of duty, Carlyle placed his confidence in 'great men'. *On Heroes and Hero-Worship* (1841), *Past and Present* (1843) and the *History of Frederick II of Prussia* (1858–65) suggested that only the tough-minded leader-dictator could translate the Social Ideal into action, through compulsion if necessary.

Rather than rely on the strong-armed 'Hero', Matthew Arnold used an urbane, lucid prose style to champion liberal-humanist values. With its calm, reflective manner and breadth of reference to high culture, Arnold's writing embodied the principles he felt best for guiding the dull middle class. *Essays in Criticism* (1865/88) and *Culture and Anarchy* (1869) advanced literature as the basis for 'civilizing' the individual and harmonizing society because its interpretation required the qualities which reason, fact and materialism neglected: flexibility and open-mindedness, perceptiveness and fine discrimination. Sensitivity and 'justness of spirit' ([1865] 1910: 157) would counteract the prejudice, smugness and complacency of the bourgeois 'Philistine'.

Ruskin used the analysis of art as the basis for cultural criticism in *Modern Painters* (1843–60) and *The Stones of Venice* (1851–3). His ornate, sententious and, at times, almost poetic prose style pointed up the debased nature of any society that ignored its own inequalities and failings. Ruskin also urged improvement by appealing positively to the patriotism and moralistic fervour of his readers. Arguing that only a spiritually sound society could generate great art, he urged the nation to rediscover the value of self-sacrifice, obedience and self-discipline. Gradually, Ruskin focused his efforts on social reform, in both his writing and his practical enterprises (like engaging his Oxford students in a road repair programme). By criticizing the evils of self-interest in Victorian industrial society, he contributed significantly to early socialist thought. *Unto this Last* (1860), for example, urged more equitable wealth distribution, while *The Crown of Wild Olive* (1866/73), *Time and Tide* (1867) and *Fors Clavigera* (1871–84) dealt with the degradation of labour when profit, not craftsmanship, became the sole criterion of worth.

John Henry Newman hated the impact of materialism and secularism on the spirituality of the nation. Politically, the Catholic Newman was conservative, distrusting liberal democracy and opposing extension of the franchise. But he was also acutely sensitive to the intellectual and moral impoverishment of the establishment, perceptible (for Newman) in its prejudice against Catholicism and its scepticism about the supernatural. In the main, Newman's classically balanced, elegant prose asserted the importance of religious faith to the renewal of individuals and nation. *Essay on the Development of Christian Doctrine* (1845), *The Present Position of Catholics in England* (1851), *Sermons Preached on Various Occasions* (1857) and *An Essay in Aid of a Grammar of Assent* (1870) defended the Roman Catholic position through wit and eloquence, as well as scholarly research. However, *The Idea of a University* (1873) made the greatest impact as cultural criticism, raising questions about a university's purpose and the value of a liberal education. The Victorian reform of Oxford and Cambridge universities had a secular basis, emphasizing specialist research and training and modern fields of study. But Newman's ideal academy prioritized teaching and the development of morally enlightened 'gentlemen'-leaders, capable of reforming both the mind and the manners of a world detached from its spiritual anchor.

Notwithstanding the renown of male 'sage' writers, a strong Victorian women-of-letters tradition brought a female perspective into public life, even though women could not participate directly in the formation of policy and legislation. The radical Harriet Martineau, for example, produced a number of instructive books for the Society for the Diffusion of Useful Knowledge, including *Illustrations of Political Economy* (1832–4) and *Illustrations of Taxation* (1834), which mediated abstract social theory through fictionalized tales. Martineau also promoted progressive thinking about social systems through her condensed translation of Comte's writings on Positivism. Frances Power Cobbe (1822–1904) addressed sociological issues from a more rebellious position. Drawing on her personal philanthropic activities with the poor, especially women, she campaigned on behalf of the marginalized and exploited. Her polemical writing covered such topics as the exclusion of women from universities, the lack of legal redress against violent husbands ('Wife-Torture in England', 1878), women's legally enforced dependence on men (*Criminals, Idiots, Women and Minors?*, 1869) and the unjust divorce laws.

Women's roles and rights permeated the work of most Victorian female prose writers. Sometimes this was the explicit theme, as in Dinah Mulock Craik's *A Woman's Thoughts about Women* (1858). But work in many disciplines asserted the complexity of women as beings of intellect, passion and imagination with a right to lead useful lives outside the home. For example, Anna Jameson's art history (*Legends of the Madonna*, 1852) contributed to campaigns for female empowerment that gathered force mid-century. Of course, not all women writers who engaged in public comment espoused values that we would recognize today as feminist. The early 'conduct' books of Sarah Stickney Ellis (1799–1872), including *The Women of England, their Social Duties and Domestic Habits* (1839) and *The Daughters of England* (1842), advised young women on appropriate behaviour in

the home and in marriage, thereby endorsing such patriarchal principles as the separate spheres for women and men,
and the 'natural' basis of male authority and female depen-
dency. Isabella ('Mrs') Beeton's (1836–65) *The Book of
Household Management* (1859–61), a substantial guidebook to
running the middle-class family home, enforced traditional
views of class as well as gender since servants were said to
welcome firm discipline, simple rewards, and a general air of
superiority on the part of mistress and master – a highly
paternalistic view of the weaker 'lower orders'. The debates
of gender politics continued in women's prose throughout
the period. In a series of acid journalistic pieces, Eliza Lynn
Linton (1883) ridiculed the modern 'girl of the period' who
demanded emancipation, a position which earned Linton
the hostility of such 'New Woman' novelists as Sarah Grand
(1854–1943).

Travel writing
Travel writing offered exciting access to the unfamiliar, but it
also contributed to Victorian self-fashioning by reinforcing
a sense of British superiority and sophistication. Fanny
Trollope's success with *Domestic Manners of the Americans* (1832)
largely stemmed from her disdainful depiction of the
United States as a naïve, gauche and vulgar nation. Harriet
Martineau was more analytical in *Society in America* (1837) and
Retrospect of Western Travel (1838), but equally critical of
American failings, and – it has to be said – also very popular.
Dickens followed suit with *American Notes* (1842) (that offended
his North American readership) and *Pictures from Italy* (1846)
(that pandered to British prejudice about Mediterranean
Continentals and Catholics in roughly equal measure).
Spectacular accounts of adventure in the wilderness achieved
similar effects by indicating the extensive spread of Victorian
civilization, and the British military and economic prowess
that made it happen. David Livingstone's *Missionary Travels
and Researches in South Africa* (1858), Henry Morton Stanley's
How I Found Livingstone (1872) and John Hanning Speke's
Journal of the Discovery of the Source of the Nile (1863) are typical,

though in style they range from the high-minded and worthy, through the gossipy and adventurous, to the scholarly.

Certainly, some examples of the genre were low-key. Robert Louis Stevenson's accounts of his Spanish meanderings (*Travels with a Donkey in the Cevennes*, 1879) and honeymoon in an abandoned mining camp in California (*The Silverado Squatters*, 1883) are essentially impressionistic, charming and picturesque sketches. Nonetheless, a number of travel writers offered enriched understanding of other societies. Alexander William Kinglake's record of journeys to Turkey, Syria, Egypt and Palestine (*Eothen: or Traces of Travel Brought Home from the East*, 1844) and Austen Henry Layard's report of archaeological expeditions (*Nineveh and Its Remains*, 1849) depended on the romance of the unfamiliar to stir empathy for ancient cultures. Layard's aim was furthered through the Assyrian statuary he sent back to the British Museum, subsequently inspiring Dante Gabriel Rossetti's poem, 'The Burden of Nineveh' (1886). The explorer Richard Burton (1821–90) was even more open to alien cultures, although his writing, like *First Footsteps in East Africa* (1856), had all the superficial traits of a standard imperialist adventure: strongly plotted with emphasis on bold derring-do, suspense and danger. Burton's unorthodoxy was particularly evident in *Personal Narrative of a Pilgrimage to Al-Medinah and Meccah* (1855–6), which dramatizes the thrill of discovery *and* rebellion. Burton was the first English person to visit these holy sites, but did so disguised as a Moslem. His translation of the *Arabian Nights* (1885–8) was equally iconoclastic. Privately printed, it retained the explicit sexual material of the original, but benefited from an insider's immersion in the language, idiom and beliefs of another culture.

Not all Victorian travel writing was sympathetic to the culturally Other. The construction of the 'East' as morally unrestrained, sensual, infantile and barbaric permeated many run-of-the-mill travel books. However, the best works enticed readers to respond less judgementally to cultural difference. Amelia Edwards' immensely detailed and readable illustrated account of her journey, *A Thousand Miles up the Nile*

(1877), had a special appeal to would-be tourists, though it was also a scholarly analysis of ancient Egyptian civilization as traced through its monumental remains. Mary Kingsley (1862–1900), Charles Kingsley's niece, wrote in a lively and amusing way about her African travels. Nonetheless, despite the stylistic informality, *Travels in West Africa* (1897) and *West African Studies* (1899) challenged stereotypical Victorian constructions of the 'Dark Continent', forcing readers to adjust their preconceptions about African landscapes and peoples.

Life writing

Curiosity about 'other' lives also accounts for the fascination with biography and autobiographical writing. We know a number of unremarkable Victorians, such as the country parson, Robert Francis Kilvert, only because they yielded to the impulse of the age to record their daily observations in diaries and journals. However, the process by which an individual struggled to maturity was the main preoccupation of Victorian life writing; readers especially savoured insight into the beliefs motivating the subject and explaining achievement. John Stuart Mill's *Autobiography* (1873), for example, traced his intellectual formation, including his prodigious learning and breakdown, and his realization that feeling added depth to his understanding of self, others and society. Newman's *Apologia pro Vita Sua* (1864), often hailed as one of the most influential autobiographies of the period, represented his religious development as a coherent 'evolution' from an Evangelical upbringing through High Anglicanism and, finally, conversion to Catholicism.

Some autobiographical writing was more concerned with the external influences which shaped a personality. Anthony Trollope's *An Autobiography* (1883) discreetly suggested that childhood unhappiness could spur attainment (in his case, in both the civil service and literature). While the book contains material on Trollope's working methods as a novelist, it is a particularly interesting example of the Victorian belief in self-help and persistence. On the other hand, in *Father and Son* (1907) Edmund Gosse (1849–1928) depicted his

Victorian up-bringing as one of crisis and conflict rather than steady progress to success. Treating his life-story as representative of late-Victorian culture, Gosse rewrote generational strife as the struggle between an outmoded mid-Victorian righteousness and a modern resistance to religious and social dogmatism. Wilde's *De Profundis* (1905), written during imprisonment for homosexual offences, began as a reproachful letter to Lord Alfred Douglas who had been involved in his downfall. In its final form, the work remade Wilde's image, transforming him into cultural scapegoat and humble penitent ennobled by suffering.

Life writing also fulfilled a high-minded duty to encourage and guide others. Harriet Martineau's *Autobiography* (1877) indicated setbacks could be overcome, while Ruskin's *Praeterita* (1885–9) traced the way a strong sense of social purpose could emerge from a personal fascination (with art, in his case). However, Ruskin downplayed many sides of his private life, including his annulled marriage and periods of mental illness. Writing *about* great men and women was similarly selective, providing information about successful self-management rather than setbacks. Especially popular was '*The Life and Times*' format which included correspondence and miscellaneous unpublished papers, as well as biographical detail and contextual information, though anything likely to disillusion readers was carefully censored. John Forster's *The Life of Dickens* (1872–4), based extensively on manuscript material and Forster's first-hand knowledge of his friend, captured Dickens's accomplishments, energy and theatricality, but was circumspect about Dickens the family man, omitting details of his relationship with the actress Ellen Ternan, for example.

Certain key biographies altered the approach to life writing. Elizabeth Gaskell's *The Life of Charlotte Brontë* (1857) marked an artistic advance, using novel-writing techniques to capture the subject from the inside. While sympathetic, Gaskell's method was critically astute and respected the role of Brontë's imagination in transforming life into art. David Masson's (1822–1907) stolid seven-volume *Life of Milton* (1859–94) lacked compelling narrative momentum, but was the first major biography of an English writer that fully researched the author's era as well as life.

The cultural importance of biography was signalled by the founding of the *Dictionary of National Biography*, under the editorship of Leslie Stephen (1832–1904). This *Dictionary* was to English lives what the *Oxford English Dictionary* was to the English language. The latter project, first published in 1884, sought to list every English word, in every sense in which it had ever been used. Its scientific approach showed language as historically specific *and* dynamic. The *Dictionary of Literary Biography* aimed, similarly, for comprehensiveness, providing well-researched, objective accounts of every notable person in the nation from earliest times to the present.

Victorian working-class life writing also existed, though it was long neglected by scholars. The best-known collection is the interview series for the *Morning Chronicle* conducted by the co-founder of *Punch*, Henry Mayhew (1812–87). In the late 1840s, he recorded the personal stories of poor Londoners. The accounts of starvation, disease and stoicism within the ranks of labourers and sweatshop workers as well as the criminal fringes gave a significant voice to a previously silent (and silenced) urban community. Collected as *London Labour and the London Poor* (1851–2), the transcriptions, though heavily edited, gained poignancy from the ordinary language of Mayhew's subjects, including their dialect, colloquialisms and trade jargon. A few working-class success stories were published, such as the *Life of Thomas Cooper, Written By Himself* (1872) and the *Life and Struggles of William Lovett in His Pursuit of Bread, Knowledge and Freedom* (1876), both of which combined Chartist radicalism with an illustration of the benefits of self-help.

Journalism: newspapers and periodicals

Victorian journalism experienced a revolution. In 1801, there were 129 publications that could be termed serials (newspapers, magazines and reviews that were produced daily, weekly, monthly or quarterly). By 1900, this number had reached 4,819, a pro-rata growth over four times that of the population (Ryan 2001: 216). Today's reader might be a little surprised by some practices. Book reviews and essays were, in the main, anonymous with attendant possibilities for 'puffing' (talking up one's own work or that of a friend) and 'log-rolling' (writing an enthusiastic review of someone else's work in exchange for a favourable review of one's own book). However, in Victorian journalism we can also spot the basis of our current press industry: aggressive advertising, pressured deadlines, rivalry over scoops and breaking news, tabloid sensationalism, even competitions with prizes (though the reward of a seven-room house for one short-story competition (Onslow 2000: 14) seems a little generous even by today's standards). Technology influenced journalistic culture by making mass print runs and distribution possible. But the marketplace was also expanded – and fragmented – by a broader spectrum of readers who craved entertainment to fill their leisure hours and information to make the most of personal potential.

General interest periodicals for the upper-middle-class reader appeared from the early 1800s. To the expensive, academic heavy-weights – *The Edinburgh Review* (1802–1929), *The Quarterly Review* (1809–1942) and *The Westminster Review* (1824–1914) – were added journals with more varied content, such as *Fraser's Magazine* (1830–82). Their popularity encouraged publishers – such as Richard Bentley – to produce their own magazines, mixing fiction and factual material to amuse and educate. These periodicals offered something for every member of the middle-class household, but they also had commercial advantages, not least by keeping publishers' names well to the fore (as in *Bentley's Miscellany*, 1837–68). Including the work of major celebrity authors lured purchasers; serialization of long novels encouraged repeat custom; and new writers could be tested without significant financial outlay.

As the range of journals expanded, hierarchies emerged. New opinion-forming serials, such as *The Fortnightly Review* (1865–1934) and *The Nineteenth Century* (1877–1950), presented erudite, scholarly discussions of serious political, religious, social and artistic topics together with fiction. Their contributors included Arnold, Eliot, Pater and Ruskin. More literary periodicals, like *The Cornhill Magazine* (1860–1975), edited by Thackeray, mixed some 'higher journalism' with poetry and fiction by the likes of Trollope, Gaskell, Reade, Browning, George MacDonald and Swinburne. Dickens's *Household Words* (1850–9) and *All the Year Round* (1859–95) applied the model to weeklies intended for the family. As proprietor, editor and frequent contributor, Dickens offered accessible fiction, light verse, editorializing observations on topical issues, and essays popularizing new knowledge in many fields. Cheaper, lighter magazines favoured the eye-catching, rather than the thought-provoking. For upper-working- and lower-middle-class readers, the inexpensive *Tit-Bits* (1881–1920) specialized in competitions, correspondence, cheeky anecdotes, extracts and abundant advertising, while the more sophisticated *Belgravia* (1866–99) and its rival, *Argosy* (1865–87), combined short articles and fashion with racy fiction. The latter two journals had, interestingly, female editors – the sensation novelists, Mary Elizabeth Braddon and Mrs Henry Wood. Both spotted the commercial potential of such journalism, but ensured their periodicals retained an aura of decorum.

The notorious newspaper editor, W. T. Stead (1849–1912), was less fastidious about offending polite sensibilities, as is evident in his article on child prostitution, luridly entitled 'Maiden Tribute of Modern Babylon' (1885). He used shock tactics – amazing scoops, eye-catching headlines and provocative campaigning pieces – to increase the circulation and impact of *The Pall Mall Gazette* (1865–1923). Stead understood the power of mass-audience newspapers and magazines, arguing that they rightly represented *and* shaped public opinion. Matthew Arnold, for one, deplored this 'New Journalism' as sentimental and prurient writing produced by 'feather-brained' reporters for equally empty-headed 'new voters, the *democracy*' (1977: 202). Yet even the elite had their sensational serials. Coterie 'little magazines' designed to appeal to the avant-garde reader with aesthetic, erotic and decadent tastes burgeoned in the 1880s and 1890s, with such titles as *The Century Guild Hobby Horse* (1886–92), *The Savoy* (1896) and *The Yellow Book* (1894–7), notorious for its mocking, titillating illustrations by Aubrey Beardsley and its morally ambivalent writing.

Niche marketing was another feature of Victorian journalism. Children's magazines were very successful, although staid and worthy in our terms. *Aunt Judy's Magazine* (1866–85) promoted an evangelical, educational and practical line. *The Boys' Own Paper* (1879–1967), and its companion *Girls' Own Paper* (1880–1908), both established by the Religious Truth Society, instilled upright, patriotic values. Women with traditional attitudes were likely to choose the *Englishwoman's Domestic Magazine* (1852–77), edited by Isabella Beeton and her husband, while radical feminists would appreciate Barbara Bodichon's *English Woman's Journal* (1858–64). Religious magazines intended for specific denominations had a dedicated readership throughout the nineteenth century, but leisure interests also created market openings for themed periodicals, such as the *Ladies' Magazine of Gardening* (1842) and *Feathered World* (for the keeper of caged birds). *The Art Journal* (1862–1911) and *The Magazine of Art* (1878–1902) boasted an international circulation that spread knowledge of contemporary artists and aesthetic tastes.

With advances in printing technology, the illustrated newspaper became the vogue. The middle-brow *Illustrated London News* (1842–1988) is the best known, but others, such as *Cassell's Illustrated Family Paper* (1867–1930), were targeted at a less prosperous audience. *Cassell's* was one of a long line of self-help educational magazines that developed a print culture for the masses and owed much to *The Penny Magazine* (1832–45), founded by the Society for the Diffusion of Useful Knowledge. They offer a fascinating insight into working-class aspirations. The banner headings on the title page of *The Penny Magazine* – 'The Poor Mans [sic] Guardian' and 'The March of the Intellect' – emphasized self-improvement. The cover illustrations, featuring a sailor, chimney sweep and gardener among others, all avidly reading an issue, specified the intended readership: those who had already bought into the middle-class cult of social advancement through knowledge and personal effort. Journalism, like many prose genres of the period, enacted mainstream Victorian assumptions at the same time as it challenged and disrupted them.

LITERARY MOVEMENTS

Introduction

Three Victorian literary 'movements' – authors whose shared aims and style suggest a single, coherent artistic vision – are worthy of note: the Pre-Raphaelite Movement, the Aesthetic and Decadent Movement and New Woman fiction. In their time, these literary circles seemed artistically and culturally radical. Whether conscious collaborators like the Pre-Raphaelites, loose networks like the Aesthetes and Decadents, or authors related by a common stance on female emancipation as embodied in the 'New Woman', the members of these movements shared one important feature: through their work, they attacked the dull mediocrity of convention. For them, literature enabled writer and reader to see life anew.

The Pre-Raphaelite Movement

In 1849, the English art world was scandalized by the paintings of a mysterious group signing itself 'P. R. B'. The 'Pre-Raphaelite Brotherhood', whose founding members in 1848 included Dante Gabriel Rossetti, William Holman Hunt and John Everett Millais, opposed traditional notions of beauty and artistic decorum. The naturalistic portrayal of sacred and legendary figures (modelled on family and friends), the distorted perspective of a flat and foreshortened picture-plane, the scenes from literary or religious narratives often associated with an outmoded Catholic past, mediaeval iconography, hard-edged drawing, luminous primary colours and minute, realistic details (down to the dirt under the fingernails of St Joseph in Millais' *Christ in the House of His*

Parents, 1850) affronted an audience accustomed to the idealized grace, sentimentality and soft shading favoured by
European painters since Raphael.

Shock was what the Brotherhood intended. The seven-
member group believed that English art could only be revital-
ized by revolution: a dramatic return to the fresh, intensely felt
artistry that characterized the (largely religious) work of early
Italian artists. Instead of imitating Old Masters and their stale
rules, Rossetti and his circle aimed at the highest degree of
exactitude in the representation of 'Nature', however that was
to be defined. John Ruskin praised this sincerity and fidelity to
truth when he defended their work against charges of pseudo-
Catholic mediaevalism and barbaric technique. By 1852, the
group had started to disintegrate. Nonetheless, they had made
such an impression that Pre-Raphaelitism remained an
important style long after the Brotherhood had ceased to function. A second generation of enthusiasts, led by William
Morris and Edward Burne-Jones, ensured the Movement
enjoyed an influence well into the 1880s.

Dante Gabriel Rossetti was also an accomplished poet who
transposed Pre-Raphaelite visual principles to writing. The
most obvious characteristics of early Pre-Raphaelite literature are evident in contributions to the Brotherhood's short-
lived magazine, *The Germ: Thoughts towards Nature in Poetry,
Literature and Art* (1850). Rossetti's short story, 'Hand and Soul',
introduced his philosophy of art: 'In all that thou doest, work
from thine own heart, simply' ([1850] 1984: 31). 'The Blessed
Damozel', his poem about a pure maiden in heaven, put this
theory into practice with parallels to Pre-Raphaelite painting:
archaic diction and courtly love allusions, a vaguely religious
mystical symbolism and sensuous descriptive detail. However,
this work and 'My Sister's Sleep' in the same journal showed
that Pre-Raphaelitism was as much about rebellion as mediaevalism. The ambivalence of the focalizer in each poem
meant that neither text clearly endorsed Christian belief,
despite pious subject matter. Religious orthodoxy had no
more place in Rossetti's conception of the Pre-Raphaelite
spirit than did clichéd artistic conventions.

A number of significant Victorian poets were associated with Rossetti as a loose Pre-Raphaelite literary circle, including his sister Christina, William Morris and Algernon Swinburne. Rossetti's mistress and wife, Elizabeth Siddal (1829–62), also produced a limited range of work attracting recent scholarly attention. While these poets would all claim strict fidelity to nature as their distinctive principle, their differences and the changes in Rossetti's own style suggest Pre-Raphaelitism is a protean concept. Swinburne, for example, was very much an outlying figure, his experimentation with sound and rhythm being far more adventurous than that of other Pre-Raphaelites. He avoided crisp precision and detail in imagery, and replaced mediaeval and Christian symbols by allusions to pagan and classical Greek sources. Unlike the Rossettis and Morris, he positively *cultivated* a reputation for offensiveness, with blasphemous attacks on Christianity and Victorian sexual orthodoxy.

Christina Rossetti's poetry employed Pre-Raphaelite stylistic features quite subtly and with different thematic emphases. The rich sensuous detail, vaguely mediaeval setting and incantatory verse form of 'Goblin Market' (1862) could be deemed Pre-Raphaelite, but the devout Christian angle of the poem with its conflict between sensual pleasure and the benefits of renunciation and self-sacrifice is not. Despite her High Anglican vision, Rossetti's poetry, including the sonnet sequence 'Monna Innominata' (1881), is Pre-Raphaelite in its melancholy tone, in its challenge to sentimental pieties (about women and faith, for example), and in its faithful rendition of spiritual and psychological anguish.

William Morris was much closer to the original intentions of the Brotherhood when he employed mediaeval forms and subjects in his poetry. In keeping with the Pre-Raphaelite commitment to 'minute detail' and 'absolute uncompromising truth' (Ruskin 1861: 181), Morris rejected an idealized Middle Ages in *The Defence of Guenevere and Other Poems* (1858), favouring fidelity to the historical record. 'The Haystack in the Flood', for instance, rewrote chivalry as a brutal power-game, and 'The Defence of Guenevere' was 'uncompromising' in the emotional depth of its characterization. No submissive Victorian wife or repentant fallen woman, Guenevere made a strong case for the beauty of passionate love. However, mystical dream poems in the same volume, notably 'The Blue Closet' and 'The Tune of Seven Towers', illustrated the new directions of Pre-Raphaelitism. While the settings, characters and verse form echoed mediaeval folktales and eerie ballads, the narrative remained obscure. Instead, through esoteric, elusive images, each poem evoked a strange mood that unsettled and intrigued. Morris's later socialist prose fantasy, *A Dream of John Ball* (1886–7), has a mediaeval setting, but both this and the utopia, *News from Nowhere* (1890), are not really Pre-Raphaelite, though they do emphasize the worth of creativity and the importance of rebellion against orthodoxy (as expressed in social and economic structures).

Dante Gabriel Rossetti's changing style confirms that Pre-Raphaelitism constantly redefined itself. The dramatic monologue, 'Jenny' (1870), employed irony and accurate detail to challenge conventional attitudes to the prostitute as a despicable woman, and the ballad, 'Sister Helen' (1853), evoked Pre-Raphaelitism through its mediaeval setting and verse form and its dramatic representation of elemental passions, notably jealousy and revenge. Yet, in its depiction of thwarted desire, the poem pointed forward to the emphasis on sensual love, dream-like effects and morbid tone characteristic of Rossetti's later visual and literary work. These qualities can be traced in the ornate and impressionistic sonnet-sequence, *The House of Life* (1870). Some of the poems, including 'Nuptial Love', employed meticulous sense details metaphorically, giving a 'sacred' status to erotic experience. Others, such as 'A Superscription' and 'Body's Beauty', subordinated pictorial effects altogether, favouring esoteric emblems, archetypes like the femme fatale, and complex personifications.

The initial harsh response to Pre-Raphaelite work was largely because it challenged expectations. Gradually, helped by Ruskin's endorsement and the enthusiasm for the Gothic revival, the Pre-Raphaelite manner became a sign of cultural modishness. However, as Pre-Raphaelite visual and literary work became sensually explicit and more overtly concerned with impression, effect and mood rather than narrative, audiences once more grew restive. Pre-Raphaelitism in its late-Victorian phase, particularly as practised by Rossetti, became associated with another controversial artistic movement: that of Aestheticism, or the 'art-for-art's-sake' Movement, and its later development, Decadence.

Aestheticism and Decadence

Victorian understanding of Pre-Raphaelitism *and* Aestheticism was shaped by a number of critical interventions. The most notorious of these was 'The Fleshly School of Poetry', Robert Buchanan's review of Rossetti's *Poems* (1870). The essay principally attacked Rossetti, but Swinburne, Morris, the (homosexual) painter, Simeon Solomon, and even Tennyson at his most 'epicene' were swept into the same category of 'trash' (1871: 335, 339). Buchanan's critique of 'the fleshly gentlemen' linked the work of the Pre-Raphaelite Rossetti to the 'art-for-art's-sake' doctrine of Aestheticism through a shared delight in rich, sensuous detail. By concentrating on form rather than content, both movements made 'poetic expression . . . greater than poetic thought' (335). Buchanan detected something unmanly and 'nasty' in the erotic frankness of Rossetti's imagery, and at the same time deemed the Aesthete 'an intellectual hermaphrodite' (338, 335). This gendered imagery constructed both Pre-Raphaelite poetry and Aestheticism as unnatural.

Such implications of abnormality ensured that Aestheticism was interpreted, from the start, as a rebellion against morality. Because it rejected a dogmatic function for art, it seemed a self-indulgent and perverse philosophy, devoid of serious social purpose and obliquely connected to a sexually ambiguous, possibly homosexual, sub-culture. Gilbert and Sullivan's Savoy opera, *Patience* (1881), mocked Aestheticism along these lines, especially through the languid 'Fleshly Poet', Reginald Bunthorne – a caricature of such notorious 'celebrity' Aesthetes as Wilde, Swinburne and the painter, James Whistler. Bunthorne urged his followers to 'walk down Piccadilly with a poppy or a lily in your mediaeval hand', fixing forever in the audience's mind some 'peculiar' association between Aestheticism, Pre-Raphaelitism and affected young men (Gilbert 1994: 165).

Gilbert and Sullivan's teasing parody may have been light-hearted, but the many serious criticisms of Aestheticism condemned its celebration of sensuous beauty and its disdain for orthodox moral, social and political ideals. Throughout the 1870s and 1880s, the essayist and Oxford don, Walter Pater, emerged as the 'voice' of Aestheticism. In critical essays and his philosophical romance, *Marius the Epicurean* (1885), he argued that the pleasurable sensations aroused by beautiful art were more important than moral enlightenment. The 'Conclusion' to his influential *Studies in the History of the Renaissance* (1873) suggested that, in the modern world of doubt, isolation and flux, the love of beauty for its own sake was the only way to give meaning and purpose to existence: 'To burn always with this hard, gem-like flame, to maintain this ecstasy, is success in life' ([1873] 1893: 251). This controversial advice further associated Aestheticism with the dangerously unorthodox: decidedly pagan and homoerotic in its sensibility, *The Renaissance* repudiated Victorian morality and a Christianity that disdained the body.

By the late 1880s, Aestheticism had been reshaped by a French influence: Symbolism. Its chief exponent on the Continent was the poet Charles Baudelaire (1821–67), whose art of 'strange disease and sin' was publicized in Britain by Swinburne (Hyder 1972: 33). Stylistically, Baudelaire anticipated the twentieth-century Imagists, treating the material world as a network of symbols. Philosophically, he luxuriated in decadence; since nature was fallen, what was *un*natural, perverse and artificial was preferable. Symbolism appealed to the English *fin-de-siècle* generation of poets, including W. B. Yeats (1865–1939), who felt alienated from traditional social and artistic values and wanted new sensations to eclipse their own world-weariness. Arthur Symons, John Gray (1866–1934), Lionel Johnson, Ernest Dowson and Oscar Wilde embraced French-style Decadence as a poetic mode suited to a closing age: 'ingenious, complicated . . . full of shades and of rarities . . . taking colours from all the palettes, notes from all the keyboards' (Symons 1920: 36).

Revelling in dandyism, elegant artifice, delicious vices and curious sensations, the Decadent poets dedicated their lives, like their art, to the cultivation of exquisite pleasures. *Silverpoints* (1893), John Gray's collection of original poems and translations of Paul Verlaine, Baudelaire, Stéphane Mallarmé and Arthur Rimbaud, was in physical terms *the* most characteristically Decadent production of the 1890s. The slim volume completely defied traditional expectations, celebrating its own preciousness through fine visual design and minimalism. Elegant covers enclosed thick, handmade paper on which there was more margin than poetry, while an impressionistic unity was suggested through images of wistfulness and despair, linked by association rather than logic.

In practice, Decadent output showed little consistency in style and theme, though the tone was uniformly cool and allusive. Ernest Dowson delighted in painful pleasures – whether observing the 'Nuns of the Perpetual Adoration' (1896) with 'calm, sad' ennui, or feeling 'desolate and sick of an old passion' in 'Non Sum Qualis Eram Bonae sub Regno Cynarae' (1896) ('I am not as I was under the reign of good Cynara'). On the other hand, Wilde's play *Salomé* (1893), about the beheading of John the Baptist at the behest of Herod's stepdaughter, was a self-consciously stylized revel in sordid horror, hingeing on overripe sexuality, cruelty, perversion and lust. Arthur Symons associated the 'disease' of the Decadent Movement with the enticing intoxications of the bohemian underworld. His impressionistic, understated poems celebrated charm where others found despair: in the impoverished busker ('The Street-Singer', 1889), in artifice ('Maquillage', 1892), and in the befuddled 'dance of mere forgetfulness' of 'The Absinthe-Drinker' (1892). The languorous style of Lionel Johnson's 'The Dark Angel' (1895) imported Decadent sensationalism and sexual ambiguity into the traditional religious poem of temptation and resistance. 'Michael Field' (the pseudonym of the lesbian writing team of Katherine Bradley and Edith Cooper) hovered uneasily under the Decadent banner, connecting love and cruelty and employing erotic imagery in a provocative manner ('La Gioconda', 1892). Yet they nervously withdrew one of their poems from *The Yellow Book*, the most notorious of the Aesthetic and Decadent magazines of the 1890s. In that journal Max Beerbohm's (1872–1956) 'A Defence of Cosmetics' (1894) simultaneously embraced and satirized Decadent artifice, summing up the defiance and self-consciousness central to the movement.

New Woman fiction

New Woman fiction of the 1880s and 1890s was a literary phenomenon that emerged from social, rather than artistic, concerns, and opposed traditional views about female sexuality and gender roles. The term, 'New Woman', coined by the novelist, Sarah Grand, did not come from a specific political movement, but acknowledged Victorian women's campaigns for improved social rights (in employment and education, for example). It also reflected late Victorian debates about marriage and the disappointments and suffering often hidden behind the façade of domestic respectability. This was not a matter just for those of 'advanced' views. Following Mona Caird's (1858–1932) suggestion in 'Marriage' (1888) that love would be better fostered by a 'free' voluntary union between man and woman (rather than an economically driven, permanent contract no better than prostitution), 27,000 correspondents answered the *Daily Telegraph's* question: 'Is Marriage a Failure?' (Richardson 2001: 184). With feminists arguing that wedlock was a stifling emotional straitjacket more likely to create female neurosis than to relieve it, Victorian womanhood seemed on the brink of a revolution in which autonomy would replace a culture of dependence and conformity.

New Woman fiction described a version of this modern femininity, incorporating women's achievements in reform but also signalling their aspirations for the future, and particularly their desire for personal empowerment. The imagined construct known as the New Woman rejected conventional respectability, embraced economic, sexual and educational independence, and declined to consider marriage and maternity as the only 'natural' route to fulfilment. Those with conservative views about women's role mercilessly mocked this model. Cartoonists, sketch writers and essayists reduced her to something freakish and 'mannish', a figure to be disdained and pitied. The anti-feminist, Eliza Lynn Linton, sneered at the disruptive, insane and man-hating 'shrieking sisterhood' (1883, II: 64). Margaret Oliphant, among others, attacked New Woman fiction for its depiction of marriage as an arbitrary social arrangement that exercised sexual tyranny over women.

Combining narratives of courtship and marriage with the strong Victorian tradition of social critique in fiction, New Woman novels were characterized less by uniformity of style than by the sympathetic portrayal of the New Woman 'type'. Men could certainly author this fiction. Hardy's rebellious, free-thinking Sue Bridehead in *Jude the Obscure* (1895) was considered a neurotic version of the New Woman, and the debates about the morality of marriage in George Gissing's *The Odd Women* (1893) placed this novel within the movement. Perhaps the most successful of all New Woman novels, *The Woman Who Did* (1895), was also by a male writer, Grant Allen (1848–99). The conclusion of this work – the suicide of the heroine – is typical of New Woman plots. Only tragic outcomes, such as death or psychological destruction, seemed 'real' destinies for rebellious, freedom-loving women in a confining culture. By thwarting an idealistic woman's bid for independence, these novels illustrated the cruel power of the existing social system. Olive Schreiner's (1855–1920) *The Story of an African Farm* (1883) and Mona Caird's *The Daughters of Danaus* (1894) followed this pattern. Usually sexual relationships and marital difficulties occasioned a woman's defeat, a point in accord with feminist criticism of the day, such as Caird's *The Morality of Marriage* (1897).

Of course, many New Woman novels also proposed an antidote to such domestic poison: a social structure that could accommodate women's needs and talents, as Sarah Grand imagined in *The Beth Book* (1897), an autobiographical study of escape from a corrupt husband. Sometimes this utopian vision was combined with sensationalism to underline the horrors of the sexual double standard and the 'abnormality' of traditional beliefs about gender difference. Grand's best-selling *The Heavenly Twins* (1892), for example, employed shocking subjects (syphilis, mental damage and cross-dressing) and an unusual structural device – the juxtaposition of fictional 'case-studies' – to make this point. At the other end of the stylistic spectrum, George Egerton (the pseudonym of Mary Chavelita Dunne) (1859–1945) combined rhythmical prose, psychological reflection, fantastic reveries and epiphanic moments to put the New Woman case. Her collections of proto-modernist short stories – *Keynotes* (1893), *Discords* (1894), *Symphonies* (1897) and *Fantasias* (1898) – were published by John Lane, the avant-garde firm responsible for *The Yellow Book*. This clear association with Decadence indicated Egerton's anti-conventional attitudes and ensured her notoriety as both artist and feminist. Yet, even in the New Woman context she was unusual, being one of the few writers who successfully imagined women's regeneration. Following natural instincts and drives enabled a woman to reconnect with her mysterious soul: 'the eternal wildness, the untamed primitive savage temperament that lurks in the mildest, best woman' ([1893] 1983: 22).

Like the Pre-Raphaelites, Aesthetes and Decadents, New Woman writers participated in the battles for intellectual and artistic authority that characterized the period. Whether condemned as immoral, or hailed as the expression of modernity, each of these literary movements shows how authors tried to apply the Victorian energy for progress and reform to their own artistic practice. Moreover, their legacy goes beyond individual works. All three movements show the creative importance of a sceptical, open-minded interrogation of conventional assumptions, artistic or social. The continuous dialogue of a society with itself is the real guarantor of the freedoms and fulfilment which these writers sought – and one of the most fascinating aspects of Victorian literature and culture.

3

Critical Approaches

HISTORICAL OVERVIEW

The Victorians and criticism

At the outset of the Victorian period, critics assumed that the visual and literary arts had a didactic role. Art conveyed moral truth, and thus contributed to the improvement and cohesion of the social body, as well as to the intellectual and spiritual nourishment of the individual. As John Ruskin suggested, ethics and aesthetics were related: the best art conveyed 'the greatest number of the greatest ideas . . . [and] exercises and exalts the faculty by which it is received' (1903: III: 92). Early Victorian criticism concentrated, therefore, on the ideas and values embedded in the work, usually considering formal elements – beauties of style, structure and technique – only insofar as they made content attractive and accessible. In this way, Victorian criticism served as a regulatory mechanism, policing subjects that art presented to the public gaze. Works that challenged favoured beliefs and traditional forms – from *Jane Eyre* (1847) to Swinburne's poetic blasphemies – were denigrated as artistic failures. Such criticism endorsed the legitimacy – and hence the 'truth' – of the ideas conveyed. Moreover, as the conduit of moral teaching, the artist was also judged in terms of sincerity and intellect, 'fineness' of perception and 'abundance' of 'moving thoughts' (Mill 1981: 361).

However, Victorian criticism gradually changed, in line with shifting views about intellectual authority. When religious doubt and the pressures of secular life shattered consensus, the relationship between critic and public was subtly altered. Instead of policing artistic work on behalf of the community, criticism took a leading role in determining the values needed by a confused society. Humanist critics, such as Matthew Arnold, argued that high culture, especially literature, offered the one reliable basis for consolation and enlightenment because it focused on the inner dimension of human experience. In 'The Function of Criticism at the Present Time' (1865), Arnold installed the critic as the moral guide and guardian of the nation, ready 'to learn and propagate the best that is known and thought in the world' ([1865] 1910: 38). Although mid-Victorian critics still made evaluative pronouncements, they accepted Arnold's challenge to be cultural reformers, seeking 'what will nourish us in growth toward perfection' (40). To accomplish this end, they required the capacity to observe dispassionately, to analyse, compare and discriminate.

By the late-Victorian period, however, new theories of art and beauty blurred the boundaries between the making and the interpreting of an artistic work. Aestheticism, savouring beautiful form for its own sake, presented both a problem and an opportunity. The Aesthetes rejected a functional view of art. As Oscar Wilde claimed, '*[a]ll art is quite useless*' ([1890/1] 2005: 168). Since the reinforcement of moral values was irrelevant to artistic practice and to the merit of a work, criticism that focused on the moral utility of art was meaningless. Instead, Aesthetic critics like Wilde and Pater focused on conveying the pleasurable effects of art at conscious and unconscious levels. The successful critic was no longer the person who could identify and evaluate the ideas encoded in a work, but the sensitive and responsive observer who, like any artist, was inward-looking, striving solely to 'know one's impression as it really is, to discriminate it, to realize it distinctly' (Pater [1873] 1893: x).

By the end of the century, a new approach was added to the Victorian critical repertoire. The impressionist Aesthetic critic demonstrated how a work stimulated the imagination to shape its own version of 'truth'. An excellent example can be found in Pater's analysis of Leonardo da Vinci's painting, 'Mona Lisa'. Pater does not try to excavate some underlying meaning of the work, nor speculate on the circumstances of its production; nor is he concerned with an analysis of craftsmanship. Instead, he *recreates* the painting, finding a striking new image to serve as an analogy for the effect of the painting on his own emotional and aesthetic sensibilities: 'She is older than the rocks among which she sits; like the vampire, she has been dead many times, and learned the secrets of the grave' ([1873] 1893: 132). This imaginative interaction of creative and critical faculties is central to Wilde's construction of both artist *and* interpreter in his essay, 'The Critic as Artist' (1888).

Critical approaches in the twentieth century

Criticism of the Victorians – both their culture and their literature – began in the twentieth century with a very palpable hit. Lytton Strachey's (1880–1932) heretical *Eminent Victorians* (1918), a collection of four essays each devoted to a representative pillar of the Victorian establishment, revealed a pompous, self-satisfied, hypocritical and base society. His portraits of Cardinal Manning, Thomas Arnold, Florence Nightingale and General Gordon revealed smooth operators intent on self-promotion and careful of appearances, but devoid of high principles and intellectual honesty. By demolishing these icons of respectability, Strachey established a new myth of Victorian dullness and moral duplicity. Read today, his book seems full of acid resentment and spitefulness, employed mainly to show the liberated sophistication of his own generation. Nonetheless, his interpretation of the period shaped the general perception of Victorian culture for many decades to come.

Early scholarly attention to Victorian literature took the same line, discarding many authors as unworthy, minor and drab. In truth, the Victorian canon constructed in criticism between 1900 and the 1950s largely reflected the make-up and tastes of university departments at this time (white, male, heterosexual, secular, liberal-humanist and entranced by the stylistically adventurous or 'modern'). Victorian dramatists, women writers, working-class writers, popular culture and most prose writers outside the limited literary 'canon' were generally discounted. On the whole, fiction was less valued than poetry, the latter being considered the most intellectually challenging of the literary arts. Literary historians, such as George Saintsbury (1896) and David Cecil (1934), surveyed Victorian writing as a straightforward mirror of its age. They considered authors in their historical chronology, establishing traditions, influences and continuities and pointing out relationships between genres, themes and styles. Meanings – both literary and cultural – were generally felt to be unproblematic, and criticism took an 'appreciative' line, assuming that all right-thinking readers would understand the view of life that such work presented.

Canon formation – establishing the hierarchy of important Victorian writers and works – also seemed largely unproblematic. It centred largely on 'great men of letters' (and a few female writers who matched the patriarchal criteria). Authors who had a prominent public role in speaking *to* the Victorian nation and who seemed representative of high culture were particularly valued: Tennyson, Arnold, Browning, Dickens, Eliot and Hardy. A few critics saw Victorian writing as a response to complex historical and political circumstances, notably the French scholar, Louis Cazamian (1904), who investigated fiction that explicitly engaged with the 'Condition of England'. Many, following in Strachey's footsteps, read both fiction and poetry as symptomatic of Victorian hypocrisy, repression and narrow-mindedness.

In the first half of the twentieth century, literary criticism tended to take Victorians at their own word. Rather like many Victorian critics, F. R. Leavis (1936; 1948) focused judgementally on the moral weight and sonority of an author's ideas. Just as the Victorians proclaimed the functional value of artistic truth, Leavis and his followers rated nineteenth-century writers largely for their capacity to refine the sensibility of readers and provide values by which to live. Leavis assessed the moral seriousness of particular authors on the basis of his personal intuition and liberal-humanist philosophy. The authors he valued were said to express timeless 'universal' insights into human nature and propose ethical frameworks for an age stripped of religious belief. What emerged was an elitist interpretation of Victorian culture and its literature that rendered it remarkably homogeneous. While attention was given to the ways in which Victorian writers addressed social change, criticism at this time did not analyse the ideological assumptions informing literary works, nor consider the specific historical conditions governing its creation and reception.

Mid-twentieth century, however, a more complex view of Victorian writing emerged, due largely to the increasing interest in psychoanalytic and historical approaches. The 'alienated' Victorian, torn between the desires of the body and the demands of the soul, replaced the Victorian as prophet or hypocrite (Miyoshi 1969). New attention to neglected writers, such as Arthur Hugh Clough, Robert Louis Stevenson, Emily Brontë and Gerard Manley Hopkins, extended the canon (Miller 1963). Analysis of the untidy contradictions, ambiguities and tensions revealed in the techniques and themes of these writers encouraged a new mapping of nineteenth-century cultural forms. Victorian literature no longer delivered a cohesive and consistent cultural viewpoint. Individual authors, like Browning, who had previously been read as earnest and robust now appeared anxious and uncertain.

Raymond Williams (1958; 1970) also advanced criticism by introducing Marxist readings of Victorian literature and culture. Although earlier scholars had placed nineteenth-century writing in a simple historical framework, Williams was one of the first to consider how Victorian literature was shaped by and circulated particular ideological viewpoints. Novels about industrialization, for example, now seemed much more ambiguous, with authors simultaneously celebrating this progressive economic phenomenon and condemning its attendant evils. Williams and the critics he influenced deepened understanding of what it meant to interpret literature through historical and cultural contexts.

CURRENT ISSUES AND DEBATES

New theoretical approaches in the last quarter of the twentieth century have considerably altered the critical approach to Victorian writing. Feminism, New Historicism (and cultural materialism) and postcolonial theory have introduced new subjects of study as well as new analytical methods. Overall, this theoretical refreshment has revealed the political and cultural complexity of Victorian literature, establishing that the relationship between literary form, history and 'life' is problematic. The ideological basis of Victorian artistic representations has become a central point of debate.

Important interventions from feminist criticism have transformed the Victorian canon, beginning with Elaine Showalter (1977) who mapped the neglected, but significant, 'alternative' tradition of women's writing in the period. Sandra M. Gilbert and Susan Gubar (1979) analysed the psychological conflicts apparent in the work of female authors, reading literary form as an expression of writers' anxiety *and* protest about the restrictive definitions of femininity available in a patriarchal society and literary tradition. The wider outgrowth from feminism – gender theory – has enriched understanding of Victorian cultural politics and incorporated further marginalized authors into the canon, in terms, for example, of *fin-de-siècle* culture (Showalter 1991), popular fiction (Bristow 1991) and periodical literature (Fraser *et al.* 2003). There has been extensive research on the representation of alternative models of masculinity and sexuality, showing the way in which particular literary forms encoded dissident identities for select Victorian audiences. Eve Kosofsky Sedgwick (1985), for example, traced the different literary expressions of Victorian homophobia and homoeroticism. The application of gender theory to Victorian women's poetry (Leighton 1992) and 'New Woman' writing (Ledger 1997; Richardson 2001) has generated new readings and recovered neglected authors.

Historicist criticism has altered understanding of the relationship between Victorian literature, its cultural context, and the material conditions affecting its production and circulation. The intersection of literature with the language and ideas of other Victorian discursive fields, like science (Beer 2000) and medicine (Shuttleworth 1996), has generated new interdisciplinary scholarship and shown how contentious subjects (like the body) are anxiously written into and out of particular works. Historicism has also challenged earlier assumptions about the straightforward, transparent nature of specific forms, genres and modes, like realism and the Gothic, as well as revising ideas about the 'truthfulness' of literary language. This critical approach, inflected by the work of Michel Foucault and exemplified by D. A. Miller (1988) and Mary Poovey (1995), has drawn attention to the operation of Victorian literature as a cultural form, acting in conjunction with a range of other non-literary cultural 'texts' to disseminate specific ways of thinking and to inscribe, or resist, particular ideological positions. Historicist and gender approaches have also been effectively combined to show the sophistication of writing previously discounted by literary scholars, such as sensation fiction (Pykett 1992).

Although postcolonial theory primarily focuses on the writing of colonial and postcolonial cultures, it too has influenced the reading of Victorian literature produced by the 'home' culture. Like feminist and historicist criticism, postcolonial theory draws attention to literary discourse as ideologically shaped and understood. Patrick Brantlinger (1988) and Daniel Bivona (1990) have demonstrated how Empire inhabits Victorian texts silently and circumspectly, from *Jane Eyre* to *Alice's Adventures in Wonderland* (1865) and

Dickens's *The Mystery of Edwin Drood* (1870). Postcolonial theory has encouraged scholars to consider how far even radical Victorian literature routinely legitimizes imperial assumptions about cultural differences and racial origins.

Such approaches continue to bear fruit in a wide range of new topics and fields of study. Working-class writing, by its nature more ephemeral and less well preserved and documented, is steadily being recovered. The relationship between narrative methods, cultural crisis and 'popular' genres is prompting reassessment of domestic romance, detective writing and early science fiction. Alternative Victorian ideas about identity, at personal and social levels, are being uncovered through interdisciplinary research into Victorian literature and nineteenth-century science, psychology, medicine, law, economics and religion. Contemporary criticism has also attached new academic value to Victorian prose and to the 'history of the book'. The latter field involves the study of the material production and dissemination of writing, as well as the reading habits of different social groups. One important area is the relation between writing style, commercial imperatives and the format in which a book is published. Another is the way Victorian writers communicated their intentions through the physical design and publication format of a volume, as well as through its coded contents.

Undoubtedly, recent developments in critical and cultural theory have introduced new themes and topics into the study of Victorian literature. Above all, however, these new approaches have reinserted Victorian literature *into*, rather than alongside, cultural history. Literary works are no longer regarded simply as mirrors of the past, or as entertaining adjuncts to the 'business' of a society. Literature is now firmly embedded as one of many dynamic cultural forms of the Victorian era, producing and being produced by its historical moment. As twenty-first century scholars, we can never 'recover' its meaning for a Victorian reader; but we can collaborate to produce new interpretations that are culturally inclusive, and deepen our sense of connection with a fascinating age.

4

Resources for Independent Study

Chronology of Key Historical and Cultural Events
Glossary of Key Literary Terms and Concepts
Further Reading and Resources

CHRONOLOGY OF KEY HISTORICAL
AND CULTURAL EVENTS

1829 Catholic Emancipation Act
Invention of the first steam locomotive
Founding of Metropolitan Police Force
1830 Opening of Liverpool and Manchester
Railway
Tennyson, *Poems, Chiefly Lyrical*
1831 Darwin's voyage on *The Beagle*
1832 First Reform Act
Tennyson, *Poems*
1833 Oxford Movement commences
Abolition of slavery in British Dominions
1834 Poor Law Amendment Act (New Poor Law)
Fire destroys Parliament buildings
1836 Dickens, *The Pickwick Papers*
1837 Accession of Queen Victoria
Dickens, *Oliver Twist*
1838 Founding of Chartism with *The People's Charter*
1839 Chartist riots
Photography processes publicized (Henry Fox Talbot)

Carlyle, *Chartism*
1840 Penny post introduced
Marriage of Queen Victoria to Prince Albert
1841 Boucicault, *London Assurance*
1842 Further Chartist riots
Mudie's Select Circulating Library founded
Browning, *Dramatic Lyrics*
1843 Wordsworth becomes Poet Laureate
Theatre Act abolishes patent monopoly system
Carlyle, *Past and Present*
Dickens, *A Christmas Carol*
Ruskin, *Modern Painters* (volume 1; continued 1846, 1856, 1860)
1844 Factory Act restricts hours of work for women and children
Chambers, *Vestiges of the Natural History of Creation*
1845 John Henry Newman converts to Roman Catholicism
Irish Potato Famine begins
Franklin expedition to the Arctic
Disraeli, *Sybil*
1846 Repeal of the Corn Laws
Dickens, *Dombey and Son*
Strauss, *The Life of Jesus Critically Examined* (trans. George Eliot)
1847 Chloroform used as anaesthetic
A. Brontë, *Agnes Grey*
C. Brontë, *Jane Eyre*
E. Brontë, *Wuthering Heights*
Tennyson, *The Princess*
Thackeray, *Vanity Fair*
1848 Public Health Act (also 1872, 1875)
Revolutions in Europe demanding reform
Formation of the Pre-Raphaelite Brotherhood
A. Brontë, *The Tenant of Wildfell Hall*
Gaskell, *Mary Barton*
Marx and Engels, *Communist Manifesto*
Mill, *Principles of Political Economy*
Thackeray, *The History of Pendennis*

1849   C. Brontë, *Shirley*
Dickens, *David Copperfield*
Macaulay, *History of England* (vols 1 and 2; continued 1855)

1850   Roman Catholic ecclesiastical hierarchy restored in England
Tennyson becomes Poet Laureate
The Germ published by the Pre-Raphaelites
Barrett Browning, *Sonnets from the Portuguese*
Kingsley, *Alton Locke*
Tennyson, *In Memoriam*

1851   The Great Exhibition
Barrett Browning, *Poems*
Mayhew, *London Labour and the London Poor*
Ruskin, *The Stones of Venice* (vol. 1; continued 1853)
Stowe, *Uncle Tom's Cabin*

1852   New Houses of Parliament opened
First free public library opened in Manchester
Dickens, *Bleak House*
Thackeray, *The History of Henry Esmond*

1853   Arnold, *Poems*
C. Brontë, *Villette*
Gaskell, *Ruth*
Yonge, *The Heir of Redclyffe*

1854   Crimean War; charge of the Light Brigade at Balaclava
Dickens, *Hard Times*
Gaskell, *North and South*
Patmore, *The Angel in the House* (completed 1861)

1855   Livingstone discovers Victoria Falls
R. Browning, *Men and Women*
Dickens, *Little Dorrit*
Kingsley, *Westward Ho!*
Tennyson, *Maud and Other Poems*
Trollope, *The Warden* (first in Barsetshire series)

1857   The Indian Mutiny
Matrimonial Causes Act
Barrett Browning, *Aurora Leigh*

Gaskell, *Life of Charlotte Brontë*

1858 Abolition of property qualification for MPs, enabling working-class men to stand

Clough, *Amours de Voyage*

Morris, *The Defence of Guenevere and Other Poems*

1859 Mrs Beeton, *Book of Household Management* (serial publication)

Collins, *The Woman in White*

Darwin, *On the Origin of Species*

Eliot, *Adam Bede*

Fitzgerald, *The Rubáiyát of Omar Khayyám*

Mill, *On Liberty*

Smiles, *Self-Help*

Tennyson, *Idylls of the King* (completed 1885)

1860 Dickens, *Great Expectations*

Eliot, *The Mill on the Floss*

1861 Civil War in America (1861–5), resulting in abolition of slavery

Founding of Morris & Co. (interior design)

Wood, *East Lynne*

1862 Source of Nile discovered

Braddon, *Lady Audley's Secret*

Meredith, *Modern Love*

C. Rossetti, *Goblin Market and Other Poems*

1863 First Underground Railway journey in London

Whiteley's Department Store opens in London

Kingsley, *The Water-Babies*

Le Fanu, *The House by the Churchyard*

Taylor, *The Ticket-of-Leave Man*

1864 Dickens, *Our Mutual Friend*

Browning, *Dramatis Personae*

Newman, *Apologia pro Vita Sua*

Trollope, *Can You Forgive Her?* (first in Palliser series)

1865 Antiseptic used in surgery

Arnold, *Essays in Criticism* (1st series)

Carroll, *Alice's Adventures in Wonderland*

Swinburne, *Atalanta in Calydon*

1866 Hyde Park riots for the right of mass assembly

Parliament petitioned for female suffrage
Permanent telegraph cable link to North America
Eliot, *Felix Holt, The Radical*
Swinburne, *Poems and Ballads* (1st series)

1867 Second Reform Act (virtually all male urban-dwellers enfranchized)
Robertson, *Caste*

1868 Trades Union Congress formed
End of transportation for felonies
R. Browning, *The Ring and the Book*
Collins, *The Moonstone*

1869 Girton College (for women) founded at Cambridge
Suez Canal opened
Arnold, *Culture and Anarchy*
Mill, *The Subjection of Women*

1870 First Married Women's Property Act
Education Act (established school districts)
D. G. Rossetti, *Poems*

1871 Religious tests abolished at Oxford, Cambridge and Durham
Stanley finds Livingstone
Eliot, *Middlemarch*

1872 Secret Ballot Act
Butler, *Erewhon*
Hardy, *Under the Greenwood Tree*

1873 Home Rule League founded in Ireland
Mill, *Autobiography*
Newman, *The Idea of a University*
Pater, *Studies in the History of the Renaissance*

1874 First Impressionist Exhibition in Paris
Hardy, *Far from the Madding Crowd*
Thomson, *City of Dreadful Night*
Trollope, *The Way We Live Now*

1876 Queen Victoria becomes Empress of India
Telephone patented by Alexander Graham Bell
Eliot, *Daniel Deronda*
Hopkins, 'The Wreck of the Deutschland'

1877 Phonograph perfected by Thomas Edison

1878   Lady Margaret Hall (for women) founded at Oxford
University of London admits women to degrees
Electric street lighting introduced in London
Hardy, *The Return of the Native*

1879   Gilbert and Sullivan, *The Pirates of Penzance*

1880   Education Act (education up to the age of 10 made
compulsory)
Greenwich Mean Time adopted

1881   Henry James, *Portrait of a Lady*
Gilbert and Sullivan, *Patience*

1882   Second Married Women's Property Act
Phoenix Park terrorist murders in Dublin

1883   Schreiner, *The Story of an African Farm*
Stevenson, *Treasure Island*

1884   Third Reform Act (most males now entitled to
vote)
Fabian Society formed
Oxford English Dictionary
Jones, *Saints and Sinners*

1885   Socialist League formed
Criminal Law Amendment Act, including the
Labouchere Amendment
Motor car invented
Dictionary of National Biography
Haggard, *King Solomon's Mines*
Moore, *A Mummer's Wife*
Pater, *Marius the Epicurean*

1886   Liberal Party splits on Irish Home Rule question
Haggard, *She*
Hardy, *The Mayor of Casterbridge*
Stevenson, *The Strange Case of Dr Jekyll and Mr Hyde*;
Kidnapped

1887   'Bloody Sunday' Trafalgar Square riots against
unemployment
Doyle, *A Study in Scarlet* (first Sherlock Holmes story)
Hardy, *The Woodlanders*

1888   Kodak box camera invented
Jack the Ripper murders in Whitechapel, London

Arnold, *Essays in Criticism* (2nd series)
Kipling, *Plain Tales from the Hills*
Ward, *Robert Elsmere*
1889 London Dock Strike
Symons, *Days and Nights*
1890 Morris, *News from Nowhere*
Wilde, *The Picture of Dorian Gray* (extended book form, 1891)
1891 Education Act (elementary education free)
Gissing, *New Grub Street*
Hardy, *Tess of the D'Urbervilles*
1892 Keir Hardie elected as first Independent Labour MP
Ford builds first car
Grand, *The Heavenly Twins*
Kipling, *Barrack-Room Ballads*
Shaw, *Widowers' Houses* (performed)
Wilde, *Lady Windermere's Fan* (performed)
1893 Egerton, *Keynotes*
Gray, *Silverpoints*
Pinero, *The Second Mrs. Tanqueray*
Wilde, *A Woman of No Importance* (performed)
1894 Caird, *The Daughters of Danaus*
Kipling, *The Jungle Book*
Shaw, *Arms and the Man* (performed)
The Yellow Book first published
1895 First radio transmission by Marconi
Moving images produced by French cinematograph
Allen, *The Woman Who Did*
Hardy, *Jude the Obscure*
Wells, *The Time Machine*
Wilde, *The Importance of Being Earnest; An Ideal Husband* (performed)
1896 *Daily Mail* founded
Housman, *A Shropshire Lad*
Jones, *Michael and His Lost Angel*
Wells, *The Island of Dr Moreau*
1897 National Union of Women's Suffrage Societies founded

Aspirin discovered
Stoker, *Dracula*
1898 James, *The Turn of the Screw*
Wells, *The War of the Worlds*
1899 Boer War in South Africa (until 1902)
1900 Labour Representation Committee formed (becomes
Labour Party in 1905)
Freud, *The Interpretation of Dreams*
1901 Death of Queen Victoria
Kipling, *Kim*

GLOSSARY OF KEY TERMS AND CONCEPTS

Aestheticism (see Chapter 2)

The principles of 'art for art's sake' (*l'art pour l'art*), adapted by British writers from the theories of the French novelist and poet, Théophile Gautier (1811–72). Aesthetes rejected a moralistic, functional role for art, arguing that it had no obligation but to be beautiful, and that the artist should stand apart from society recording exquisite feelings and vision, however unorthodox these might seem. Walter Pater was the most influential exponent of Aestheticism in Victorian Britain, especially in *Studies in the History of the Renaissance* (1873), *Marius the Epicurean* (1885) and *Appreciations: with an Essay on Style* (1889). Aestheticism had strong associations with late Pre-Raphaelitism and 1890s Decadence.

Bildungsroman (see Chapter 2)

Originally, a German genre of realist fiction, exemplified by Johann Wolfgang von Goethe's *Wilhelm Meister's Apprenticeship* (1795–6). Based on the development of an individual from childhood to young adulthood, it emphasizes individual endeavour and progress, as in Dickens's *Great Expectations* (1860–1) and Charlotte Brontë's *Jane Eyre* (1847). Concentrating on apprenticeship and education (in the broadest sense of these words), the Bildungsroman represents the *process* by which an individual is formed, but also the *portrait* of the ideal adult who emerges. These are reinforced through themes (such as 'rags-to-riches'), a chronological plot (illustrating change in response to experience), minor characters (offering alternative models of behaviour), narrators (commenting on mistakes and triumphs) and settings (signalling tests and crises essential to development). Some critics argue the genre reflects and responds to Victorian gender ideology, distinguishing between the 'male' Bildungsroman (featuring a boy who learns to take responsibility in the family and wider world) and the 'female' Bildungsroman (focusing on a girl's gradual discovery of her own needs and capabilities).

Commodification

The process by which artefacts, people and their activities become valued purely as objects of exchange and economic worth. Karl Marx identified commodification as a damaging feature of capitalism, creating inequality by reducing the employer–employee relationship to the impersonal buying and selling of labour. Thomas Carlyle objected to this 'Cash-nexus' (*Chartism*, 1839), as did many 'Condition of England' novelists (see Chapter 2), including Elizabeth Gaskell in *Mary Barton* (1848).

Dandyism

Generally, a man's fastidious preoccupation with elegant dress and fashionable manners, associated with the Regency courtier, George 'Beau' Brummell. By the 1890s, Dandyism implied a philosophy, defined by Oscar Wilde in *The Picture of Dorian Gray* (1890/1) as 'an attempt to assert the absolute modernity of Beauty' ([1890/1] 2005: 278). The elegant Victorian dandy styled himself a sophisticated 'intellectual' aristocrat, standing above the mainstream and practising life itself as an art form. As well as flamboyant (sometimes effeminate) costumes and mannerisms, a 'modern' contempt for middle-class views, refined tastes, a graceful idleness and wit characterized the dandy's pose, which Wilde both embraced and mocked through characters like Lord Goring in his play, *An Ideal Husband* (1895).

Decadence
An outgrowth of Aestheticism, flourishing in the 1890s, and finding beauty and pleasure in sensuousness, artifice, the exotic and the abnormal. Heavily influenced by Charles Baudelaire's poems, *Les fleurs du mal* (*The Flowers of Evil*, 1857), and by Joris-Karl Huysmans's (1848–1907) novel, *A rebours* (*Against Nature*, 1884), the movement upheld the autonomy of art in the face of society's decline. The Decadent achieved fulfilment by cultivating sensations arising from extreme and bizarre experiences, sometimes including sexual perversity. The poet and essayist, Arthur Symons, produced an important analysis of the movement of which he was a part in *The Decadent Movement in Literature* (1893). His poems of the London demi-monde, *Days and Nights* (1889) and *London Nights* (1895), display Decadence as 'a new and beautiful and interesting disease' ([1893] 1968: 903).

Fin de siècle
Literally, end of century. The term refers not only to the historical decade of the 1890s, but also to feelings of cultural anxiety and ambivalence typical of that time. Associated with the sense of spiritual and moral decline identified by Max Nordau in *Degeneration* (1895), the term is often applied to the spirit of ennui and malaise in Decadent literature (see Chapter 2) and art.

Mammonism
The Victorian middle-class worship of money and commercial success, denounced, for example, by Carlyle in *Past and Present* (1843).

Materialism
In Victorian culture, not primarily a concern with acquiring material goods, but a belief that the physical world and laws

of matter constitute the sole reality. Materialism rejects God, immortality and the supernatural, suggesting that human life is a purely 'material' phenomenon that can be explained, controlled and improved by scientific study. The phenomenon of materialism shows how science replaced religion as a source of knowledge in the nineteenth century, even though many Victorians, such as Tennyson (*In Memoriam*, 1850), worried that materialism reduced humanity to an animal species, struggling for survival in the face of an indifferent Nature, 'red in tooth and claw'.

Mrs Grundy

A priggish character who never appears, but is repeatedly invoked as the 'busy-body' representative of 'proper' standards, in Thomas Morton's play, *Speed the Plough* (1798). Victorians referred to the character (or to 'Grundyism') to indicate the power of censorious, conservative public opinion, obsessed with the 'respectable'. Wilkie Collins's *The Law and the Lady* (1875) attacks such attitudes.

Naturalism

A movement in nineteenth-century French fiction, associated especially with Émile Zola (1840–1902). Neither idealizing reality, nor acknowledging anything beyond the material world, Naturalist fiction projects a rational, scientific stance through its detached, clinical voice; careful observation of detail; dispassionate analysis of the human condition, including the sleazy, the degrading and the taboo; and use of natural and social laws to explain behaviour. By introducing such topics as violence, suicide and unbridled lust, Naturalists expose the grim reality behind the reassuring bourgeois myth of social progress. Unlike realism (to which it seems superficially similar), Naturalism is essentially pessimistic. Its characterization and plotting suggest individuals lack control, being at the mercy of impersonal forces, including biology, environment, heredity and economics. George Moore and George Gissing adapted Naturalism for British audiences.

New Woman (see Chapter 2)

A character type and cultural 'model' representative of a particular feminist viewpoint in the late Victorian period. New Woman novels, including *A Superfluous Woman* (1894) by Emma Frances Brooke (1859–1926) and *A Yellow Aster* (1897) by 'Iota' (Kathleen Mannington Caffyn) (1855–1926), reject the repressive roles imposed on Victorian women, arguing for emancipation in all spheres of life, from sexuality to education and work. Free-thinking (usually agnostic or atheist) and well read in the literature of female protest, the New Woman character resists convention in many ways, from 'rational' dressing (avoiding restrictive corsets and styles that deformed the body) to pursuing erotic fulfilment outside marriage. Intelligent, articulate and self-reliant, these characters courageously proclaim their independence though they are frequently destroyed, a plot outcome suggesting the implacable power of society in determining women's destiny.

Philistinism

Not the Biblical Philistines, but adapted from the German word *philister*, meaning a person who is not a university student. Matthew Arnold uses the term in *Essays in Criticism* (1865) and *Culture and Anarchy* (1869) for the Victorian middle-class indifference, or even hostility, to the life of culture, of beautiful things and of the mind. To them, he contrasts the aristocratic class ('Barbarians', with their love of sports and manners) and the working-class 'Populace'. Some characters in Dickens's *Hard Times* (1854) and Elizabeth Gaskell's *North and South* (1854–5) display Philistine attitudes, including an over-valuation of wealth and respectable appearances.

Realism (see Chapter 2)

The dominant mode in Victorian fiction, based on the view that art 'imitates' life. Victorian realist novels use many narrative techniques to convey an unromanticized picture of 'real' experience: a focus on the everyday and on social diversity; detailed sense description; chronological cause-and-effect plotting; familiar settings; linguistic accuracy such as dialect; and referential, rather than abstract and symbolic, language. Formal realism (where the very style of the narrative mimics real life, such as a journal, autobiography or collection of letters or documents) is a favourite device. Equally important is social realism (which attempts to convey the complexity of a sophisticated urban milieu) and psychological realism (which concentrates on the inner thoughts and feelings of the individual). Today we recognize that realism is not a neutral fictional mode. While realist novels seem to offer an unmediated 'slice of life', their strong, developing characterization, instructive narrators and tidy, closed endings represent middle-class beliefs: that individuals control their lives; that social duty can be reconciled with personal desire; and that communities are essentially organic and harmonious, provided each person keeps to their appointed and fulfilling place. George Eliot's *Middlemarch* (1871–2) is an outstanding example of the classic realist novel, but chapter 17 of her novel, *Adam Bede* (1859), is a usefully explicit statement of realist ideological assumptions.

Romanticism

A late-eighteenth- and early nineteenth-century European cultural movement embracing art, literature, politics and philosophy. Informed by belief in the power of imagination, the value of feeling and the essential goodness of human beings in their 'natural' state (the child, peasant or 'noble savage'), Romantic literature highlights the need for introspection, the value of the natural world as a conduit to the spiritual power of the universe, and the importance of individual freedom and spontaneity. Literary style, especially in second generation British Romantics like Keats, is lush and sensuous, experimental in its departure from eighteenth-century genres and forms, filled with sublime imagery and allusions to myth, folktale and legend, and sometimes mystical and ecstatic in tone. Early Victorian lyric poetry was heavily influenced by the Romantics, as evidenced in Tennyson's *Poems, Chiefly Lyrical* (1830) and *Poems* (1832).

Secularism

The governance of culture, thought and institutions by non-religious ideas. In Victorian society, spiritual principles and outlooks were gradually eroded by the loss of confidence in Christianity, the decline in the Church's importance in social affairs, and the growth of state power. By 1870, when the National Secular Society was founded, the process of secularization was well entrenched. However, many Victorians failed to distinguish very clearly between secular and 'religious' attitudes. Nominally Christian, they tended to be rather vague about supernatural doctrines, though committed to ethical values associated with Christianity.

Sensation Fiction: see Sensationalism

Sensationalism

Associated both with Victorian physiological-psychological theories about cognition and the nervous system and, more popularly, with the lurid reporting of scandalous events. 'Sensation fiction' of the 1860s, such as Wilkie Collins's *The Woman in White* (1859–60) and *No Name* (1862–3), takes its name from both meanings. The shocking crimes and social offences that form its subject reveal the secret vice beneath respectable middle-class domesticity. Its narrative techniques – involving intricate plotting, knife-edge suspense and sinister mysteries – supposedly disturb the nerves, that is, the physical, emotional, mental and moral well-being of readers. Reviewers criticized the genre for its contribution to social degeneration, fearing it would create a depraved craving for cheap literary thrills and indifference to immoral behaviour.

Symbolism

A French movement of the last half of the nineteenth century, particularly influential in Britain on Swinburne and the Decadent poets (see Chapter 2), including Arthur Symons. Taking its philosophy from Charles Baudelaire, who treated nature as a vast 'forest of symbols' in the sonnet

'Correspondances' (1857), Symbolism values imagery that reveals the poet's soul and points to a superior reality beyond the world of phenomena. Because Symbolists prefer allusion to description, metaphoric to referential language, and sometimes sound to sense, their poetry can seem evocative but also private, esoteric and even morbid.

FURTHER READING AND RESOURCES

Bibliographical and reference material

Drabble, Margaret (ed.) (1995), *The Oxford Companion to English Literature* (revised edn). Oxford: Oxford University Press. Concise biographical details for main Victorian authors, summaries of major texts, basic information on major periodicals.

Guy, Josephine M. (1998), *The Victorian Age: an Anthology of Sources and Documents*. London: Routledge. Excellent compendium of primary source material on social theory, ethics, politics and economics, the arts, gender, religion and science.

Shattock, Joanne (1993), *The Oxford Guide to British Women Writers*. Oxford: Oxford University Press. Potted biographical-critical summaries for most Victorian women writers.

Shattock, Joanne (ed.) (1999), *The Cambridge Bibliography of English Literature, Volume 4: 1800–1900*. Cambridge: Cambridge University Press. The essential bibliographical guide to all aspects of Victorian writing (and work about it).

Victorian Studies: Excellent annual bibliography of critical work.

The Year's Work in English Studies: Annual evaluative bibliography which reviews the major criticism from that year.

General: cultural context

Beckson, Karl (1992), *London in the 1890s: A Cultural History*. New York: W. W. Norton. Excellent survey of Wilde's social and intellectual context, including gay culture and Aestheticism.

Davis, R. W. and Helmstadter, R. J. (eds) (1992), *Religion and Irreligion in Victorian Society: Essays in Honour of R. K. Webb*.

London: Routledge. Includes essays on Evangelicalism, religion and science, liberal politics, gender and colonialism.

Dentith, Simon (1998), *Society and Cultural Forms in Nineteenth-Century England*. Basingstoke: Macmillan. Well-argued, informative account of conflicts and contradictions in Victorian culture (e.g. class, gender, city vs. country).

Fletcher, Ian (ed.) (1979), *Decadence and the 1890s*. London: Edward Arnold. Coverage includes Swinburne, little magazines and the term 'Decadence'.

Gilmour, Robin (1993), *The Victorian Period: The Intellectual and Cultural Context of English Literature 1830–1890*. Harlow: Pearson Educational Press. Puts major genres in contexts of historiography, science, religion, politics and aesthetics. Sophisticated discussion of 'reform' and 'time'.

Helsinger, Elizabeth K., Lauterbach Sheets, Robin and Veeder, William (eds) (1983), *The Woman Question: Society and Literature in Britain and America 1837–1883*. 3 vols. Chicago and London: University of Chicago Press. Excellent discussion of the main debates together with substantial extracts from key Victorian works.

Hoppen, K. Theodore (1998), *The New Oxford History of England: The Mid-Victorian Generation: 1846–1886*. Oxford: Oxford University Press. Valuable historical resource but assumes some historical knowledge.

Houghton, Walter E. (1957), *The Victorian Frame of Mind: 1830–1870*. New Haven and London: Yale University Press. 'Classic', accessible account of important Victorian beliefs, though now supplemented and challenged by more recent theoretical approaches.

Ledger, Sally and McCracken, Scott (eds) (1995), *Cultural Politics at the Fin de Siècle*. Cambridge: Cambridge University Press. Surveys late-Victorian fears: race, class and gender, Irish politics, the city and technology.

Mason, Michael (1995), *The Making of Victorian Sexuality*. Oxford: Oxford University Press. Challenges assumptions about Victorian sexual attitudes.

Newsome, David (1997), *The Victorian World Picture: Perceptions and Introspections in an Age of Change*. London: Fontana Press. Thematic rather than strictly chronological assessment of culture 'through' history; requires some knowledge of the period.

Parsons, G. (ed.) (1988), *Religion in Victorian Britain*. 5 vols. Manchester: Manchester University Press. Readable, comprehensive survey of Victorian religious ideas, practices and controversies.

Turner, Frank M. (1993), *Contesting Cultural Authority: Essays in Victorian Intellectual Life*. Cambridge: Cambridge University Press. Sophisticated intellectual history, including secularization and the relation of science to religion and politics.

Young, G. M. [1953] (2002), *Portrait of an Age* (2nd edn). London: Phoenix Press. Readable survey, dated but informative.

Young, Robert M. (1985), *Darwin's Metaphor: Nature's Place in Victorian Culture*. Cambridge: Cambridge University Press. 'Natural selection' as a key metaphor in Victorian intellectual life.

General: Victorian literature

Auerbach, Nina (1982), *Woman and the Demon: The Life of a Victorian Myth*. Cambridge, MA and London: Harvard University Press. Influential feminist examination of the polarized archetypes of woman in Victorian literature and art.

Bivona, Daniel (1990), *Desire and Contradiction: Imperial Visions and Domestic Debates in Victorian Literature*. Manchester: Manchester University Press. Shows how imperialist ideology shaped the domestic self-image in diverse literary works.

Brantlinger, Patrick (1988), *Rule of Darkness: British Literature and Imperialism, 1830–1914*. Ithaca, NY and London: Cornell University Press. Useful overview of changes in the ideologies of colonialism and empire.

Davis, Philip (2003), *The Oxford English Literary History, Volume 8: 1830–1880*. Oxford: Oxford University Press. Straightforward assessment of authors in context, highlighting Victorian concerns about the purpose of society and the individual.

Gilbert, Sandra M. and Gubar, Susan (1979), *The Madwoman in the Attic: The Woman Writer and the Nineteenth-Century Literary Imagination*. New Haven, CT and London: Yale University Press. Influential feminist study of the tension between confinement and liberation in the work of Emily and Charlotte Brontë, Elizabeth Barrett Browning and George Eliot.

Kaplan, Fred (1987), *Sacred Tears: Sentimentality in Victorian Literature.* Princeton, NJ: Princeton University Press. Important exploration of a central (but neglected) part of the Victorian reader's experience, focusing on Carlyle, Thackeray and Dickens.

Maynard, J. (1993), *Victorian Discourses on Sexuality and Religion.* Cambridge: Cambridge University Press. Ground-breaking consideration of the *connection* of these fields, using Clough, Kingsley, Patmore and Hardy.

Miller, J. Hillis (1963), *The Disappearance of God: Five Nineteenth-Century Writers.* London: Oxford University Press. Subtle readings of Robert Browning, Arnold, Emily Brontë and Hopkins, relating style to religious crisis.

Parker, Christopher (ed.) (1995), *Gender Roles and Sexuality in Victorian Literature.* Aldershot: Scolar Press. Includes essays on Schreiner, Edward Carpenter, Caird and Stoker.

Pittock, Murray G. H. (1993), *Spectrum of Decadence: The Literature of the 1890s.* London: Routledge. Overview of the literary culture of the period, covering key authors (Wilde, Stoker, Pater), movements (Symbolism, Decadence) and intellectual trends (anti-scientific thought).

Sedgwick, Eve Kosofsky (1985), *Between Men: English Literature and Male Homosocial Desire.* New York: Columbia University Press. Influential study of the different meanings attached to the Victorian representation of male same-sex relationships.

Sussman, H. (1995), *Victorian Masculinities: Manhood and Masculine Poetics in Early Victorian Literature and Art.* Cambridge: Cambridge University Press. Models of masculinity constructed by Carlyle, Robert Browning, the Pre-Raphaelites and, subsequently, Pater.

Tucker, Herbert F. (ed.) (1999), *A Companion to Victorian Literature & Culture.* Oxford: Blackwell. Excellent index and further-reading lists support essays packed with information on cultural attitudes and literature, organized by themes, genres and key topics.

Poetry

Armstrong, Isobel (1993), *Victorian Poetry: Poetry, Poetics and Politics*. London: Routledge. Sophisticated analysis of the moralistic and expressive elements in Victorian poetic theory and practice, with attention to Robert Browning but also to Tennyson, Swinburne, Hopkins, female and working-class poets.

Ball, Patricia (1976), *The Heart's Events: The Victorian Poetry of Relationships*. London: Athlone Press. Love and its psychological and emotional effects in the work of Robert Browning, Clough, Arnold, Patmore and Meredith.

Bristow, Joseph (ed.) (1995), *Victorian Women Poets: Emily Brontë, Elizabeth Barrett Browning, Christina Rossetti*. London: Macmillan. Feminist and historicist approaches to the female assertion of a poetic identity, plus good reading lists.

Bristow, Joseph (ed.) (2000), *The Cambridge Companion to Victorian Poetry*. Cambridge: Cambridge University Press. Thematic approach to poetry and cultural topics (e.g. science, religion and patriotism), covering major figures (e.g. Arnold, Robert Browning, Tennyson) but also neglected women poets.

Cronin, Richard, Chapman, Alison and Harrison, Antony H. (eds) (2002), *A Companion to Victorian Poetry*. Oxford: Blackwell. Good starting place for overview of styles, genres, schools, the marketplace and relevant cultural contexts across an extensive range of poets.

Edmond, Rod (1988), *Affairs of the Hearth: Victorian Poetry, Domestic Ideology and Narrative Form*. London: Routledge. Marriage, sexuality and women's role in Victorian narrative poetry.

Langbaum, Robert (1957), *The Poetry of Experience: The Dramatic Monologue in Modern Literary Tradition*. New York: Random House. Good introduction to the subtlety of the form in its Victorian manifestation.

Leighton, Angela (ed.) (1996), *Victorian Women Poets: A Critical Reader*. Oxford: Blackwell. Valuable attention to lesser known as well as major voices, plus evaluation of different theoretical approaches to women's poetry.

Pearce, Lynne (1991), *Woman-image-text: Readings in Pre-Raphaelite Art and Literature*. London: Harvester Wheatsheaf. Feminist analysis of such archetypes as the virgin and Guenevere.

Sambrook, James (ed.) (1974), *Pre-Raphaelitism: A Collection of Critical Essays*. Chicago: University of Chicago Press. Places the literary output in the context of nineteenth-century arts and culture.

Stevenson, Lionel (1972), *The Pre-Raphaelite Poets*. Greensboro: University of North Carolina. Accessible biographical-critical introduction to Rossetti and his circle.

Fiction

Abel, Elizabeth, Hirsch, Marianne and Langland, Elizabeth (eds) (1983), *The Voyage In: Fictions of Female Development*. Hanover: University Press of New England. Tracks distinctive female tradition in the Bildungsroman.

Armstrong, Nancy (1987), *Desire and Domestic Fiction: A Political History of the Novel*. New York and Oxford: Oxford University Press. Contribution of the novel to the entrenching of the middle class, through its treatment of home, family and gender.

Basch, Françoise (1974), *Relative Creatures: Victorian Women in Society and the Novel, 1837–67*, Anthony Rudolf (trans.). London: Allen Lane. Connects fiction to women's experience in the period.

Beer, Gillian (2000), *Darwin's Plots: Evolutionary Narrative in Darwin, George Eliot and Nineteenth-Century Fiction* (2nd edn). Cambridge: Cambridge University Press. Important study of Darwin's language, metaphors, plots and narrative structures (Eliot and Hardy).

Buckley, Jerome (1974), *Season of Youth: The Bildungsroman From Dickens to Golding*. Cambridge, MA: Harvard University Press. Good introduction to the genre.

Da Sousa Correa, Delia (ed.) (2000), *The Nineteenth-Century Novel: Realisms*. London: Routledge. Victorian realism in relation to class, sexuality, politics, colonization and commerce.

David, Deirdre (ed.) (2001), *The Cambridge Companion to the Victorian Novel*. Cambridge: Cambridge University Press. Good starting place for information about genres, intellectual debates and publishing conditions.

Dowling, Andrew (2001), *Manliness and the Male Novelist in Victorian Literature*. Aldershot: Ashgate. Gender politics from the perspective of masculinity (Dickens, Thackeray, Trollope and Gissing).

Feltes, N. N. (1986), *Modes of Production of Victorian Novels*. Chicago: University of Chicago Press. Relationship of publishing methods (e.g. the triple-decker) to narrative form and ideology.

Fraiman, Susan (1993), *Unbecoming Women: British Women Writers and the Novel of Development*. New York: Columbia University Press. Explores the case for the female Bildungsroman (Brontë and Eliot).

Garrett, Peter (1980), *The Victorian Multiplot Novel*. Harvard: Yale University Press. Important analysis of the formal structures, narrative methods and meanings of Victorian multiplot fictions.

Guy, Josephine M. (1996), *The Victorian Social-problem Novel: the Market, the Individual and Communal Life*. Basingstoke: Macmillan. Solid placing of these novels in their intellectual and political milieu.

Heilmann, Ann (2004), *New Woman Strategies*. Manchester: Manchester University Press. Persuasive analysis of the creative uses of political activism by Grand, Schreiner and Caird.

Ingham, Patricia (1996), *The Language of Gender and Class: Transformation in the Victorian Novel*. London: Routledge. Shows how Victorian language encoded gender and class stereotypes that major Victorian novelists resisted.

Ledger, Sally (1997), *The New Woman: Fiction and Feminism at the Fin de Siècle*. Manchester: Manchester University Press. Compares the lives of radical women to New Woman characters in Grand, Wilde, Caird, Schreiner and Stoker, suggesting some connections to dandyism and decadence.

Levine, George (1981), *The Realistic Imagination: English Fiction from Frankenstein to Lady Chatterley*. Chicago: University of Chicago Press. Argues Victorian realism was essentially experimental and related to other discursive practices, notably science and aesthetics.

Maison, Margaret M. (1961), *Search Your Soul, Eustace: A Survey of the Religious Novel in the Victorian Age*. London and New York: Sheed and Ward. *The* survey of religious fiction, with a valuable checklist of primary works.

Prickett, Stephen (1979), *Victorian Fantasy*. Hassocks: Harvester. Excellent introduction and overview.

Pykett, Lyn (ed.) (1996), *Reading Fin-de-Siècle Fictions*. London: Longman. Fiction discussed in relation to Aestheticism, Decadence, Symbolism, degeneration, early psychology, imperialism and sexuality.

Regan, Stephen (ed.) (2001), *The Nineteenth-Century Novel: A Critical Reader*. London: Routledge/Open University. Juxtaposes Victorian essays on the art of fiction and modern criticism of major nineteenth-century novels to illuminate realism.

Showalter, Elaine (1977), *A Literature of Their Own: British Women Novelists from Brontë to Lessing*. Princeton, NJ: Princeton University Press. Seminal construction of a new canon; focuses on novelists who battled against a sexually repressive culture.

Sutherland, John (1995), *Victorian Fiction: Writers, Publishers, Readers*. Basingstoke: Macmillan. Learned and readable account of the cultural, social and commercial influences on novel form and content.

Tillotson, Kathleen (1956), *Novels of the Eighteen-Forties*. Oxford: Oxford University Press. Reliable introduction to the literary, historical and social contexts of *Mary Barton*, *Vanity Fair*, *Jane Eyre* and *Dombey and Son*.

Walder, Dennis (ed.) (1996), *The Realist Novel*. London: Routledge. Accessible guide to the form, themes and historical context of realism.

Wolff, Robert Lee (1977), *Gains and Losses: Novels of Faith and Doubt in Victorian England*. London: John Murray. Comprehensive, historically contextualized analysis of fiction dealing with Victorian crises of faith.

Drama

Booth, Michael R. (1981), *Victorian Spectacular Theatre 1850–1910*. London: Routledge & Kegan Paul. Excellent overview of the drama of spectacle and sensation, including melodrama and pantomime.

Booth, Michael R. (1991), *Theatre in the Victorian Age*. Cambridge: Cambridge University Press. Comprehensive coverage of theatre practice, dramatic literature, audiences and the social and cultural context.

Gardner, Vivien and Rutherford, Susan (eds) (1992), *The New Woman and Her Sister: Feminism and Theatre, 1850–1914*. Ann Arbor, MI: University of Michigan Press. How feminists were defined on- and off-stage, in theatre management and by performers and playwrights.

Jenkins, Anthony (1991), *The Making of Victorian Drama*. Cambridge: Cambridge University Press. Victorian theatre of ideas and the social visions of Robertson, Jones, Pinero, Wilde and Shaw.

Leech, Clifford and Craik, T. W. (eds) (1975), *The Revels History of Drama in English: 1750–1880*. London: Methuen. Broad overview of theatre development from acting style to theatre design, together with sketches of major plays.

Newey, Kate (2005), *Women's Theatre Writing in Victorian Britain*. Basingstoke: Macmillan. Valuable checklist of plays and survey of central themes: home, nation, marriage and family.

Powell, Kerry (1990), *Oscar Wilde and the Theatre of the 1890s*. Cambridge: Cambridge University Press. Important placing of Wilde alongside his contemporaries to show his subversion of moral *and* dramatic structures.

Powell, Kerry (1997), *Women and Victorian Theatre*. Cambridge: Cambridge University Press. Suggests how theatre gave women an authoritative voice as actresses, theatre managers and even playwrights.

Rowell, George (1978), *The Victorian Theatre, 1792–1914* (2nd edn). Cambridge: Cambridge University Press. Useful discussion of society drama after 1860 with an excellent bibliography.

Prose

Brake, Laurel (1994), *Subjugated Knowledges: Journalism, Gender & Literature in the Nineteenth Century*. New York: New York University Press. Makes important connections between modes of production and cultural issues by focusing on literature and journalism, women's magazines in 1880s and 1890s, and biography. Valuable for both methodology and content.

Brake, Laurel and Codell, Julie F. (eds) (2005), *Encounters in the Victorian Press: Editors, Authors, Readers*. Basingstoke: Palgrave Macmillan. Excellent coverage of the role of the press in public dialogue, covering gender, class, urban issues, politics.

Fleishman, Avrom (1983), *Figures of Autobiography: The Language of Self-Writing in Victorian and Modern England*. Berkeley and Los Angeles: University of California Press. How and why Victorian sage writers and novelists rewrote the traditional autobiographical narrative of growth, loss and recovery.

Gagnier, Regenia (1991), *Subjectivities: A History of Self-Representation in Britain, 1832–1920*. New York: Oxford University Press. Scholarly comparison of autobiographies and memoirs to show the influence of class and gender on the individual's attempts to mediate between self and society.

Holloway, John (1953), *The Victorian Sage: Studies in Argument*. London: Macmillan. Relationship between philosophy and prose style in Carlyle, Disraeli, Eliot, Newman, Arnold and Hardy.

Levine, George and Madden, William (eds) (1968), *The Art of Victorian Prose*. New York: Oxford University Press. Ranges over the style of specific writers (including Macaulay, Darwin, Ruskin and Pater), the formal features of prose genres (e.g. art criticism) and different analytical methods (e.g. psychoanalytic).

Small, Ian (1991), *Conditions for Criticism; Authority, Knowledge, and Literature in the Late Nineteenth Century*. Oxford: Clarendon Press. Nineteenth-century literary criticism and its relation to other 'scientific' disciplines (Wilde and Pater).

Popular literature

Altick, Richard D. (1957), *The English Common Reader: A Social History of the Mass Reading Public, 1800–1900*. Chicago: University of Chicago Press. Pioneering survey of literacy, publishing, distribution, newspapers and periodicals, and readerships focusing on the middle and lower classes.

Boardman, Kay and Jones, Shirley (eds) (2004), *Popular Victorian Women Writers*. Manchester: Manchester University Press. Provides biographical and literary contexts for writers including Broughton, Yonge, Wood and Braddon.

Cross, N. (1985), *The Common Writer: Life in Nineteenth-Century Grub Street*. Cambridge: Cambridge University Press. Informative

account of hack-writing, including sociological background, the
marketplace, and female professional writers.

Liggins, Emma and Duffy, Daniel (eds) (2001), *Feminist Readings of
Victorian Popular Texts: Divergent Femininities*. Aldershot: Ashgate.
Surveys a wide range of popular genres in relation to feminist
and anti-feminist discourses and readerships.

Maunder, Andrew and Moore, Grace (eds) (2004), *Victorian Crime,
Madness and Sensation*. Aldershot: Ashgate. Sensation fiction,
detective stories and sensational journalism viewed through
Victorian attitudes to deviance.

Milbank, Alison (1992), *Daughters of the House: Modes of Gothic in
Victorian Fiction*. London: Macmillan. Gendered reading of
Gothic and sensational literature to characterize male and
female Gothic modes.

Pykett, Lyn (1992), *The 'Improper' Feminine: the Women's Sensation Novel
and the New Woman Writing*. London: Routledge. Interesting juxtaposition of two unorthodox fictional modes incorporating not
only feminist protest but also cultural anxiety about artistic representation and gender definitions.

Pykett, Lyn (1994), *The Sensation Novel: from 'The Woman in White'
to 'The Moonstone'*. Plymouth: Northcote House. Crisp, no-
nonsense introduction to main themes, formal features and
authors.

Robbins, Ruth and Wolfreys, Julian (eds) (2000), *Victorian Gothic:
Literary and Cultural Manifestations in the Nineteenth Century*.
Basingstoke: Palgrave. Gothic elements in a wide range of
Victorian writers, including Hopkins, the Pre-Raphaelites and
Le Fanu.

Periodicals and web resources

Periodicals

The following periodicals are essential research tools for the
student of Victorian literature and culture:

English Literature in Transition: 1880–1920
Journal of Victorian Culture
Nineteenth-Century Literature
Victorian Literature and Culture

The Victorian Newsletter
Victorian Poetry
Victorian Studies

Web resources

The Dickens Project: http://humwww.ucsc.edu/dickens/
Promotes the study of Dickens and his time via a special archive
on *Our Mutual Friend*, plus links to other electronic archives and
publications.
Literary Resources on the Net: http://andromeda.rutgers.edu/~
jlynch/Lit/
Links to online resources such as author pages, bibliographies,
e-books, new books, relevant literary societies.
Literature of the Victorian Period: www.accd.edu/Sac/English/
bailey/victoria.htm
Bibliographical information on more than 40 Victorian writers,
together with links to other relevant websites.
The Rossetti Archive: www.rossettiarchive.org/
Excellent access to visual and written material, contextual information, secondary material and links to other relevant websites.
The Victorian Web: www.victorianweb.org/
Short essays on all aspects of Victorian literature and culture, plus
links to other material and bibliographical resources. Easily
searchable.
The Victorian Women Writer's Letter Project: http://delos.lib.sfu.
ca/projects/VWWLP/
A biographical-bibliographical site dedicated to correspondence
between early and mid-Victorian women; under development,
but Anna Jameson and Harriet Martineau are the first subjects.
The Voice of the Shuttle: http://vos.ucsb.edu/
Useful, reliable gateway to online resources in Victorian literature
and culture.

References

Albert, H. R. H. The Prince Consort (1862), *The Principal Speeches and Addresses of His Royal Highness The Prince Consort*. London: John Murray.

Anon. (1851), 'Exhibition of the Royal Academy', *The Times*, 7 May, 8.

Arnold, Matthew [1865] (1910), *Essays in Criticism: First Series*. London: Macmillan.

Arnold, Matthew [1888] (1911), *Essays in Criticism: Second Series*. London: Macmillan.

Arnold, Matthew [1869] (1966), *Culture and Anarchy*, J. Dover Wilson (ed.). Cambridge: Cambridge University Press.

Arnold, Matthew (1972), 'Preface to First Edition of *Poems* (1853)', in Christopher Ricks (ed.), *Selected Criticism of Matthew Arnold*. London: New English Library, pp. 27–40.

Arnold, Matthew (1973), *The Complete Prose Works of Matthew Arnold: Volume IX: English Literature and Irish Politics*, R. H. Super (ed.). Ann Arbor, MI: University of Michigan Press.

Arnold, Matthew (1977), *The Complete Prose Works of Matthew Arnold: Volume XI: The Last Word*, R. H. Super (ed.). Ann Arbor, MI: University of Michigan Press.

Arnold, Matthew (1996), *The Letters of Matthew Arnold: Volume I: 1829–1859*, Cecil Y. Lang (ed.). Charlottesville and London: University Press of Virginia.

Atkinson, Charles Milner (1905), *Jeremy Bentham: His Life and Work*. London: Methuen.

Auerbach, Jeffrey A. (1999), *The Great Exhibition of 1851: A Nation on Display*. New Haven, CT: Yale University Press.

Bailey, Peter (1998), *Popular Culture and Performance in the Victorian City*. Cambridge: Cambridge University Press.

Basch, Françoise (1974), *Relative Creatures: Victorian Women in Society and the Novel 1837–67*, Anthony Rudolf (trans.). London: Allen Lane.

Beer, Gillian (2000), *Darwin's Plots: Evolutionary Narrative in Darwin, George Eliot and Nineteenth-Century Fiction* (2nd edn). Cambridge: Cambridge University Press.

Bivona, Daniel (1990), *Desire and Contradiction: Imperial Visions and Domestic Debates in Victorian Literature*. Manchester: Manchester University Press.

Booth, Michael R. (1965), *English Melodrama*. London: Herbert Jenkins.

Booth, Michael R. (1980), *Prefaces to English Nineteenth-Century Theatre*. Manchester: Manchester University Press.

Booth, William (1890), *In Darkest England and the Way Out*. London: Salvation Army.

Brantlinger, Patrick (1988), *Rule of Darkness: British Literature and Imperialism, 1830–1914*. Ithaca, NY and London: Cornell University Press.

Bristow, Joseph (1991), *Empire Boys: Adventures in a Man's World*. London: HarperCollins.

'A British Matron' (1885), 'A woman's plea', *The Times*, 20 May, 10.

Brontë, Charlotte [1853] (1979), *Villette*, Mark Lilly (ed.). Harmondsworth: Penguin.

Buchanan, Robert [Thomas Maitland] (1871), 'The fleshly school of poetry: Mr. D. G. Rossetti', *Contemporary Review*, XVIII, pp. 334–50.

Carlyle, Thomas [1833–4] (1937), *Sartor Resartus: The Life and Opinions of Herr Teufelsdröckh*, Charles Frederick Harrold (ed.). New York: Odyssey Press.

Carlyle, Thomas [1843] (1965), *Past and Present*, Richard D. Altick (ed.). Cambridge, MA: Riverside Press.

Cazamian, Louis [1904] (1973), *The Social Novel in England, 1830–1850: Dickens, Disraeli, Mrs Gaskell, Kingsley*, Martin Fido (trans.). London: Routledge & Kegan Paul.

Cecil, Algernon (1953), *Queen Victoria and Her Prime Ministers*. London: Eyre & Spottiswoode.

Cecil, David (1934), *Early Victorian Novelists: Essays in Revaluation*. London: Constable.

Cruse, Amy [1935] (1962), *The Victorians and Their Books*. London: George Allen & Unwin.

Cunningham, Valentine (ed.) (2000), *The Victorians: An Anthology of Poetry & Poetics*. Oxford: Blackwell.

Disraeli, Benjamin [1845] (1920), *Sybil, or The Two Nations*. London: Longmans, Green.

Disraeli, Benjamin [1870] (1975), *Lothair*, Vernon Bogdanor (ed.). Oxford: Oxford University Press.

Egerton, George [1893] (1983), *Keynotes*. London: Virago Press.

Eliot, George (1954), *The George Eliot Letters: Volume III: 1859–1861*, Gordon S. Haight (ed.). London: Oxford University Press.

Eliot, George [1859] (1980), *Adam Bede*, Stephen Gill (ed.). London: Penguin.

Engels, Frederich [1845] (1920), *The Condition of the Working-Class in England in 1844*, Florence Kelley Wischnewetzky (trans.). London: George Allen & Unwin.

Fraser, Hilary, Green, Stephanie, and Johnston, Judith (2003), *Gender and the Victorian Periodical*. Cambridge: Cambridge University Press.

Froude, J. A. [1849] (1988), *The Nemesis of Faith*. London: Libris.

The Germ [1850] (1984). Oxford: Ashmolean Museum/ Birmingham Museums & Art Gallery.

Gilbert, Sandra M. and Gubar, Susan (1979), *The Madwoman in the Attic: The Woman Writer and the Nineteenth-Century Literary Imagination*. New Haven, CT and London: Yale University Press.

Gilbert, W. S. (1994), *The Savoy Operas*. Ware: Wordsworth.

Gosse, Edmund [1907] (1922), *Father and Son: A Study of Two Temperaments*. London: William Heinemann.

Green, V. H. H. (1974), *A History of Oxford University*. London: B. T. Batsford.

Greg, W. R. (1862), 'Why are women redundant?', *National Review*, 14, pp. 434–60.

Griest, Guinevere L. (1970), *Mudie's Circulating Library and the Victorian Novel*. Newton Abbot: David & Charles.

Hardy, Thomas [1891] (1988), *Tess of the d'Urbervilles: A Pure Woman*. London: Folio Society.

Harrison, Frederic (1886), 'A few words about the nineteenth century', in *The Choice of Books and Other Literary Pieces*. London: Macmillan, pp. 417–47.

Heimann, Mary (1995), *Catholic Devotion in Victorian England*. Oxford: Clarendon Press.

Hodgson, Peter C. (2001), *Theology in the Fiction of George Eliot: The Mystery Beneath the Real*. London: SCM Press.

Hoppen, K. Theodore (1998), *The Mid-Victorian Generation: 1846–1886*. Oxford: Oxford University Press.

Houghton, Walter E. (1957), *The New Oxford History of England: The Victorian Frame of Mind 1830–1870*. New Haven: Yale University Press.

Huxley, Thomas H. (1893), 'On the physical basis of life', in *Method and Results: Essays*. London: Macmillan, pp. 130–65.

Hyder, Clyde K. (ed.) (1972), *Swinburne as Critic*. London: Routledge & Kegan Paul.

James, Henry (1935), *The Art of the Novel: Critical Prefaces*. London: Charles Scribner's.

Judd, Denis and Surridge, Keith (2002), *The Boer War*. London: John Murray.

Kaplan, Fred (1987), *Sacred Tears: Sentimentality in Victorian Literature*. Princeton, NJ: Princeton University Press.

Keble, John (1912), *Lectures on Poetry, 1832–1841: Volume I*, Edward Kershaw Francis (trans.). Oxford: Clarendon Press.

Kingsley, Charles (1899), 'How to study natural history', in *Scientific Lectures and Essays* (3rd edn). London: Macmillan, pp. 289–310.

Lacey, Candida Ann (ed.) (1986), *Barbara Leigh Smith Bodichon and the Langham Place Group*. London: Routledge & Kegan Paul.

Lambourne, Lionel (1999), *Victorian Painting*. London: Phaidon Press.

Leavis, F. R. (1936), *Revaluation: Tradition and Development in English Poetry*. London: Chatto & Windus.

Leavis, F. R. (1948), *The Great Tradition*. London: Chatto & Windus.

Ledger, Sally (1997), *The New Woman: Fiction and Feminism at the Fin de Siècle*. Manchester: Manchester University Press.

Leighton, Angela (1992), *Victorian Women Poets: Writing Against the Heart*. London: Harvester Wheatsheaf.

Linton, E[liza] Lynn (1883), *The Girl of the Period and Other Social Essays*. 2 vols. London: Richard Bentley.

Macaulay, Thomas Babington (1880), 'The people's charter', in *The Miscellaneous Writings, Speeches and Poems*. Vol. III. London: Longmans, Green, pp. 178–92.

Macaulay, Thomas Babington [1849] (1906), *The History of England from the Accession of James II*. Vol. I. London: J. M. Dent.

Maison, Margaret M. (1961), *Search Your Soul, Eustace: A Survey of the Religious Novel in the Victorian Age*. London and New York: Sheed and Ward.

[Mansel, H. L.] (1863), 'Sensation novels', *Quarterly Review*, 113, April, pp. 481–514.

Marx, Karl and Engels, Friedrich [1848] (1930), *The Communist Manifesto*. London: Martin Lawrence.

Mayhew, Henry (1971), *The Unknown Mayhew: Selections from the 'Morning Chronicle' 1849–1850*, E. P. Thompson and Eileen Yeo (eds). London: Merlin Press.

Miall, Edward (1849), *The British Churches in Relation to the British People*. London: Arthur Hall, Virtue and Co.

Mill, John Stuart (1981), 'Thoughts on poetry and its varieties', in John M. Robson and Jack Stillinger (eds), *Autobiography and Literary Essays*. London: Routledge & Kegan Paul, pp. 341–65.

Mill, John Stuart [1859] (1991), *On Liberty and Other Essays*, John Gray (ed.). Oxford: Oxford University Press.

Miller, D. A. (1988), *The Novel and the Police*. Berkeley: University of California Press.

Miller, J. Hillis (1963), *The Disappearance of God: Five Nineteenth-Century Writers*. London: Oxford University Press.

Miyoshi, Masao (1969), *The Divided Self: A Perspective on the Literature of the Victorians*. London: University of London Press.

Newman, John Henry [1873] (1964), *The Idea of a University*, Martin J. Svaglic (ed.). New York: Holt, Rinehart and Winston.

Newman, John Henry [1864] (1968), *Apologia Pro Vita Sua*, David J. DeLaura (ed.). New York: W. W. Norton.

Newsome, David (1998), *The Victorian World Picture: Perceptions and Introspections in an Age of Change*. London: Fontana Press.

Nightingale, Florence [1852] (1928), 'Cassandra', in Ray Strachey, *'The Cause': A Short History of the Women's Movement in Great Britain*. London: G. Bell and Sons, pp. 395–418.

Onslow, Barbara (2000), *Women of the Press in Nineteenth-Century Britain*. Basingstoke: Macmillan.

Oppenheim, Janet (1985), *The Other World: Spiritualism and Psychical Research in England, 1850–1914*. Cambridge: Cambridge University Press.

Oulton, Carolyn W. de la L. (2003), *Literature and Religion in Mid-Victorian England*. Basingstoke: Palgrave.

Pater, Walter [1873] (1893), *The Renaissance: Studies in Art and Poetry* (4th edn). London: Macmillan.

Pater, Walter [1893] (1896), *Plato and Platonism: A Series of Lectures* (2nd edn). London: Macmillan.

Poovey, Mary (1995), *Making a Social Body: British Cultural Formation, 1830–1864*. Chicago: University of Chicago Press.

Pykett, Lyn (1992), *The 'Improper' Feminine: the Women's Sensation Novel and the New Woman Writing*. London: Routledge.

Reynolds, Ernest (1936), *Early Victorian Drama (1830–1870)*. Cambridge: W. Heffer & Sons.

Richardson, Angelique (2001), ' "People talk a lot of nonsense about heredity": Mona Caird and anti-eugenic feminism', in Angelique Richardson and Chris Willis (eds), *The New Woman in Fiction and in Fact: Fin-de-Siècle Feminisms*. Basingstoke: Palgrave, pp. 183–211.

Robertson, David (1978), *Sir Charles Eastlake and the Victorian Art World*. Princeton, NJ: Princeton University Press.

Ruskin, John (1861), *Selections from the Writings of John Ruskin*. London: Smith, Elder.

Ruskin, John [1860] (1862), *'Unto This Last': Four Essays on the First Principles of Political Economy*. London: Waverley.

Ruskin, John (1903, 1905, 1908), *The Works of John Ruskin*, E. T. Cook and Alexander Wedderburn (eds). Vols III, XVIII, XXXV. London: George Allen.

Ryan, James (2001), 'Images and impressions: printing, reproduction and photography', in John M. MacKenzie (ed.), *The Victorian Vision: Inventing New Britain*. London: V&A Publications, pp. 215–39.

Saintsbury, George (1896), *A History of Nineteenth Century Literature, 1780–1895*. London: Macmillan.

Schlicke, Paul (1985), *Dickens and Popular Entertainment*. London: Allen & Unwin.

Sedgwick, Eve Kosofsky (1985), *Between Men: English Literature and Male Homosocial Desire*. New York: Columbia University Press.

Showalter, Elaine (1977), *A Literature of Their Own: British Women Novelists from Brontë to Lessing*. Princeton, NJ: Princeton University Press.

Showalter, Elaine (1991), *Sexual Anarchy: Gender and Culture at the Fin de Siècle*. London: Bloomsbury.

Shuttleworth, Sally (1996), *Charlotte Brontë and Victorian Psychology*. Cambridge: Cambridge University Press.

Smiles, Samuel (1859), *Self-Help; with Illustrations of Character and Conduct*. London: John Murray.

Stocking, George W., Jr. (1996), *After Tylor: British Social Anthropology 1888–1951*. London: Athlone Press.

Sutherland, John (1976), *Victorian Novelists and Publishers*. London: Athlone Press.

Sutherland, John (1989), *The Stanford Companion to Victorian Fiction*. Stanford: Stanford University Press.

Symons, Arthur (1920), *Charles Baudelaire: A Study*. London: Elkin Mathews.

Symons, Arthur [1893] (1968), 'The Decadent Movement in Literature', in Walter E. Houghton and G. Robert Stange (eds), *Victorian Poetry and Poetics* (2nd edn). Boston: Houghton Mifflin, pp. 903–09.

Taylor, W. Cooke (1842), *Notes of a Tour in the Manufacturing Districts of Lancashire*. London: Duncan and Malcolm.

Thackeray, W[illiam] M[akepeace] (1863), 'De Juventute', in *Roundabout Papers*. London: Smith, Elder, pp. 103–30.

Treuherz, Julian (1993), *Victorian Painting*. London: Thames & Hudson.

Trollope, Anthony [1883] (1974), *An Autobiography*. London: Oxford University Press.

Vaughan, Robert (1843), *The Age of Great Cities: or, Modern Society Viewed in its Relation to Intelligence, Morals, and Religion*. London: Jackson and Walford.

Wernick, Andrew (2001), *Auguste Comte and the Religion of Humanity: The Post-Theistic Program of French Social Theory*. Cambridge: Cambridge University Press.

Wilde, Oscar [1890/1] (2005), *The Picture of Dorian Gray: The 1890 and 1891 Texts*, Joseph Bristow (ed.). Oxford: Oxford University Press.

Williams, Raymond (1958), *Culture and Society 1780–1950*. London: Chatto & Windus.

Williams, Raymond (1970), *The English Novel from Dickens to Lawrence*. London: Chatto & Windus.

Wilson, A. N. (2002), *The Victorians*. London: Hutchinson.

Wolff, Robert Lee (1977), *Gains and Losses: Novels of Faith and Doubt in Victorian England*. London: John Murray.

Young. G. M. [1953] (2002), *Portrait of an Age* (2nd edn). London: Phoenix Press.

Young, G. M. and Handcock, W. D. (eds) (1956), *English Historical Documents, Volume 12i: 1833–1874*. London: Eyre & Spottiswoode.

Index